The Profitable Clinic - The Ultimate Guide to Making Money From Owning A Clinic, Spa or High End Beauty Salon!

By
Ralph Montague
The Skin Repair Group

1

The Profitable Clinic first published 2016.
This edition published 2020.
© 2020 The Skin Repair Group
ISBN 9798-651885220

Part 1 - Your Business

The Profitable Clinic - The Skin Repair Group

Part 2 - Your New Offering

Part 3 - Making This Book Work For You

The Profitable Clinic Book Series

After the huge success of The Profitable Clinic, combined with the fantastic emails and texts we have received almost daily over the last 4 years, saying how much the book has helped their clinic succeed and it was just what they needed to get themselves to the next level. We decided to ask both our readers and The Skin Repair Groups customers what they needed help with the most?

The first and biggest aspect clinic owners needed help with, wasn't a big surprise being, *"I'm nervous of not getting enough customers if I invest in a new device with you"*.

As a director of a training business that supply aesthetic devices, we of course wanted to sell more aesthetic devices, so we soon realised the best way to do this, was to help you get more customers.

Now having established the aesthetic industries biggest concern, we went away and put pen to paper (well finger to keys!) to create the best books available, to help you get more customers:

1. **The Profitable Clinic - Marketing Your Clinic.**

2. **The Profitable Clinic - Selling Your Treatments.**

3. **The Profitable Clinic - Profit Maximisation.**

4. **The Profitable Clinic - Stop Losing Your Customers.**

If you would like to further your clinic's success and profitability, you can invest in a copy of any The Profitable Clinic books, by simply visiting:

www.theprofitableclinic.co.uk

We recommend you starting with marketing your business first, then learning how to sell your treatments to your new enquiries before looking to maximising the profit you achieve on your client base and then finally applying the customer retention strategies.

Of course, the order you choose to do this is upto you and will in fact depend greatly on where you are in the business cycle. What is needed for a well-established clinic, is completely different to a medic professional or aesthetician who has just left the world of employment with bills to pay!

I hope you enjoy learning and implementing the strategies and tactics as much as I did, both learning them first hand and subsequently writing about them years later to make your clinic a roaring success...

Opening Words by Alexandra Farley

- Director of Training, The Skin Repair Group

I don't read many books, but the ones I've taken the time to read have always seemed to be one of Ralph's "amazing recommendations" and a must read if I want to progress and improve on whatever I'm doing at present, whether it's for business or personal.

I have learnt so much over the last few years working with Ralph, and this book will certainly guide you through some of the most thought proving and relevant points if wanting to make yourself even more successful in this ever growing industry.

I have seen personally how each of these techniques, or basic principles, have transformed our clinics and training company, some I agreed with, helping develop and putting in place along the way, others I really wasn't sure of, and true to his word was scared when it came to implementing.

Just remember nothing is ever as bad as it seems and nothing is ever as good as it seems, don't let the fear of putting some of the most simple and effective practices in place to make yourself and your business develop and improve. Ralph is truly inspirational and certainly has had more balls than me (literally) to get stuff done, so let him help you achieve more, be better and not just improve your business, but transform your life!

The Profitable Clinic - The Skin Repair Group

Part 1 - Your Business

11

Chapter 1

Introduction & Why I Wrote This Book...

For lots of other industries, they seem to be awash with extensive books on how to improve your business yet for Aesthetics, Beauty & Spa's very little has been published, so with my extensive knowledge built up from almost two decade's worth of experience in the industry, I thought it was time we changed this!

I didn't want this to just be another marketing book but a powerful book, completely focused towards the world of aesthetics. So even though I do cover marketing, on the most part I believe most clinics and high-end beauty salons can certainly get the feet through the door to their establishment, it's what happens next that worries me!

So quite simply, I have put together some of the best advice that I would be telling myself, if I were starting out from scratch all over again, without the experience of owning/running clinics and a training school combined with having seen many new clinics both prosper and fail.

Everything that I cover is not particularly difficult or out there but what I will say, is that sometimes it's the simplest things that can have the best impact on your business. For that reason I have tried to make it concise, so that you actually read all of it, and are not put off from implementing all the relevant actions due to you being overwhelmed by the amount of time you have to spend reviewing the book!

Over the past decade from opening up my first non-surgical cosmetic clinic back in 2005, I have had to learn things the long, painful and hard way, of what works and what doesn't! So rather than endure this very painful roller coaster ride alone, we thought we would give you our top tips for success in your business, in an ever growing and, evolving industry.

However, before we begin, I would love you all to take a quick test to see how your clinic is currently performing compared to the UK industry leaders, so we know your starting point or benchmark before we begin?

To do this, I've put together a little test for you, this will help you rate your clinics current performance and more importantly, give you guidance on where you can improve and ultimately where you need to be.

If you would like to do this test for your clinic then please simply visit:

www.theprofitableclinic.co.uk

Without further ado, here they are...

14

Chapter 2

Why Striking While the Irons Hot, Will Make You Rich!

So you have a killer marketing machine that makes the phone ring non-stop, loads of email enquiries and a constant supply of people walking through your door daily! But wait, you're not actually full, in fact most weeks' you have numerous empty slots in the diary, so what's going wrong...

Well this is simple! You're not striking while the irons hot and in fact actually sucking the momentum out of your eager potential customers!

That moment someone enquires with you, **is the single most hottest point of their desire** to have that fat freeze treatment or micro needling treatment with you. With this powerful knowledge, you need to be able to act **NOW**, you don't want this person's expectations being disappointed when they can't get hold of you or they don't hear back from you for a few days!

In this time, they can easily go from someone willing to book there and then with you, to that unreliable tyre they have been putting off replacing for months, which has now actually exploded and that £299 they were going to spend with you has now gone to Quick Fit!

The Profitable Clinic - The Skin Repair Group

The amount of reasons (excuses!) I have heard over the years for why someone who only a few days ago was super keen to book but as we didn't get back to them soon enough, turns completely cold, would have you in stitches!

In a nutshell, the longer you leave between an enquiry and contact with the potential customer, the increase in the number of externalities in the world to stop them spending that money with you over some other company, and often it's not even your competitors whose taking your money, but rather another sector that takes your money.

However, also realise that people will often enquire with a few clinics at the time of their enquiry with you and if you get back to them first, you have first pickings and as long as you can convey confidence, politeness and knowledge on that first call, if they are going to book it will be most likely with your clinic and not the person who calls a day or two later!

Finally, I think it's worth mentioning just how flaky people can be, and a lot of people will simply change their mind and for no real reason. When you ask them why they are no longer interested in having the treatment when you have called them only 2 days later, they will often just say "because", and just think how much the lead cost you in the first place...

Key Point

The quicker you get back to someone's missed call (I'd recommend an email tracking phone system so you have a list of every missed call that comes your way, more on this later) or their email enquiry, the higher your rate of booking that person in.

This can save you a fortune in advertising costs, as all of a sudden you don't need as many enquiries to fill your diary!

Create an enquiry.

Chapter 3

Multi-price Point Marketing...

Charge more and do less, it's that simple!

This was one of those steps to success where we were (shit) scared to implement and then in a matter of days it changed my business life forever! No longer was I having cash flow issues and not getting paid on time every month...

This wasn't so much a game changer, it helped us to stay in business!

Most people only offer one price point for each of the treatments they offer, for example with a Skin Micro Needling treatment using our very popular "Skin Repair Pen", you may be quoting £299, which is fine in principle but you're severely limiting your client's options. Perhaps they may be looking for a discount if they buy multiple treatments?

Let's give you an example, you could in fact quote them £349 for one area, £899 for 3 treatments (a saving of £148 in total, then rounded to just £299 per treatment) and £1,945 for 6 areas (a massive saving of £449 in total or working out at only £249 per treatment).

Now this does a few things, as previously mentioned it tells your client you are happy to reward loyalty by giving them a discount if they buy multiple treatments.

It also puts the idea in their head, as they may not have even thought of having multiple treatments and arguably best of all it anchors their mind on the last high price which now makes £349 sound dirt cheap compared to £1,494 and in fact actually the package you wanted them to go for, the £899 also sounds inexpensive when compared to £1,494.

Not forgetting there are those people in the world who always go for the best no matter how much more it is and you have just gotten yourself 6 treatments from one sales call and the money is in the bank today, helping with the all-important cash flow of a business.

Anyone need any more convincing...?

Also when given the option, nearly everybody always goes for the middle option, weird but think about it, people don't want the cheapest as they are worried it might not be any good while at the other end of the spectrum they are worried about spending too much by going for the most expensive, so what do people do, they go for the middle option, simple!

Now don't think I have finished there when it comes to pricing, we can take this even further, again using the example with skin micro needling using The Skin Repair Pen, and it's something we encourage all of our training delegates to do, is to offer a low starting price point to encourage enquiries, which can start from £249 but this is actually for small areas and then the most likely price their customers are going to be paying will in fact be £349, for larger areas! The difference these extra £50's and £100's make goes direct to your bottom line, yes NET Profit, not just turnover, when multiplied over hundreds of treatments per annum is huge and very much life changing! Or what I call "The Small Big changes".

The final element to consider while we are on the subject of pricing is those all important pounds, dropping the price from £300 to £299 or £350 to £349, trust me... it makes all the difference. It's all psychological, but it works, the reality is the treatment is still pretty much £300 but taking that £1 off the price and advertising it in the £200s makes it all the more appealing... another small but simple pricing technique.

299 instead of 300

Key Point

Give your customers a few choices when it comes to different prices as you will be surprised at how much some are willing to spend! However, whatever you do, don't give them too much choice as what often happens when we are surrounded by too many options, is that we can't make our mind up and do nothing!

Chapter 4

How to Ensure Your Clients Actually Turn Up!

Please do not underestimate just how significant this "Game Changer" is! If we didn't implement this, I would have either lost my home or be working for someone else or probably both!

I can't believe how many people are still not doing this!!! **DEPOSIT, DEPOSIT, DEPOSIT...**

No IFs, no BUTs, just do it and in 3 months' time you will be kicking yourself as to why you didn't do it sooner (and no they don't get their money/deposit back if they have the bad manners to not give you at least 24/48 hours' notice).

So you're asking yourself now, but what if it scares my customers off! Good as that's the idea, the ones who are flaky and can't commit or who will let you down, will be very nervous about paying this, and this is great as you soon get rid of the people who mess you about and make it hard to run a successful business!

This is what we want, it makes them think very hard do they really want this treatment and it's interesting as the odd few go, I think I'll leave it! How much better is it to find this out 4 weeks before the date, giving you loads of time to fill that appointment with someone else, who will actually turn up and not finding out at the very time they were supposed to be showing up while you're sat there idle...

Next your thinking, so how much deposit should I take?

Again this is simple, you should always be aiming for 50% and if they kick up a fuss and only then, let them know that you will make an exception for them and will only take 25%.

Obviously, it's up to you what you want to take and dependant on the price of the actual treatment or service you are providing but also don't forget to consider how valuable your time is. I know many people who forget this very important aspect, if your clients don't show up it's your time wasted, or maybe your staff, either way you are the one loosing out regardless of the money you thought you'd be making. Ultimately, time in this industry often directly equates to money.

Deposit taking is that simple, please don't try to make it more complicated than it needs to be!

Key Point *deposit*

If you are not taking deposits, you are a MUG!

Chapter 5

Making Sure Clients Return...

We can't take the credit for this one, a clinic we trained had been doing this for years with great results and in fact am very disappointed (and embarrassed) to admit it took us until our 9th year of business to actually nail this one! We have always over the years got in touch with clients to rebook them in, but I must admit this was very inconsistent depending on how busy we were, and not followed up a few times if we were unable to get hold of them the first time around.

We were missing out on such an amazing opportunity, these people have had great results and excellent service from us and are now very pleased customers, no further trust needs to be built up as it's there now in bundles, making booking in further treatments with us an easy sale!

Yet we weren't doing it, until we made the decision to ask every client at the end of their treatment, "when" would they like to rebook? This works on so many levels.

First, they are very pleased with everything having just had their treatment and their level of excitement is at its highest that it will ever be, then with every minute from when they leave your clinic, that enthusiasm dwindles rapidly!

You have a captive audience with no other distraction and the iron is very hot in this case. This is the perfect time to ask, so just do it, you'll be surprised that around 50% of people agree to rebook at first and when you get really good at it, you can even get this figure to around 80% of your customers. We have had days where we get 100% rebooks!

But remember, just because they have had a treatment with you today doesn't mean you don't still need to take a deposit, you will be surprised at having built up a great relationship with them during the treatment and having had them tell you how you're the best thing since sliced bread but without that deposit in a few weeks/months when it's time to come back, it may actually shock you the number of people who won't be returning unless that deposit has been taken...

If at first, you're struggling with this one for whatever reason, then perhaps start off with an offer to incentivise them to rebook, there and then. Never take off money or do it for a discount, instead always give them something extra for free e.g. free upgrade to a larger area or free cream as the value to your client for this is higher than the price you paid for it!

If you step back and think about this for a moment, it means your diary is forever 50% to 80% full in advance, which in turn means you need less customers, which in turn means you can spend less on marketing (higher profits per treatment!), that means less time on the phone booking new customers in and most amazingly, you can build up a fantastic long term relationship where they will never go anywhere else ever again (never mind mention it to all their friends how pleased they are with the excellent results they get from you).

One caveat to this though, always take a deposit, I think I already said this, didn't I? I would even ask for a high deposit to begin with, so if they then say they can't afford it today, allow them the option to pay a smaller deposit to create commitment from them.

Key Point

Straight after a treatment if they like you (which of course they will), will be one of the best opportunities you ever get EVER, to rebook your customers in!

It will also save you the cost and time of having to send them stuff in the post, write emails, make phone calls etc.!

Chapter 6

Cash is King! Turnover is Vanity, Profit is Sanity & CASH is KING!

For two reasons this is a very famous saying in almost all sectors but is not well known in aesthetics and beauty, the reason being is that a lot of people go from being a therapist or working for the NHS, to owning their own clinic or Spa overnight without much experience in-between running a business.

Cash flow management is absolutely crucial to your business as well as all the other businesses on this planet. Many profitable and successful businesses have collapsed due to lack of cash in the bank!

It's all very well making huge profits on the back of successful sales however if people aren't paying you on time or in fact paying you at all, then you could be making £10 Billion net profit and it wouldn't matter as your business would crash and burn without cash at hand and in the bank to pay staff and suppliers!

What I actually recommend is a very simple spreadsheet, split into two halves, with the left side listing all money you expect to receive in the next 8 weeks, with a description of the income (typically the names of your customers) and the amount inserted in the relevant week the money will hit your bank account.

Then on the right side of the spreadsheet, we do the same but this time for expenses.

You can then get your weekly net movement of cash position e.g. if you have income of £10,000 that week and expenses of £7,000 then you will have a net cash inflow of £3,000, this amount will then be added to your starting bank balance for the week to give you an accurate and timely record of how liquid your business is. Liquidity is key whether in business or for your own personal finances.

If you would like the spreadsheet template I have created and that my own company, The Skin Repair Group uses, please visit the link below for your free copy www.theprofitableclinic.co.uk/free-bonus-gifts

Cash flow ties in very nicely with a few of my previous points about deposits and rebooks straight after a treatment. If you are booking customers in 4 to 6 weeks in advance and they are paying you 50% deposit at the time of booking, you have an amazing business spitting out cash!

It's the type of business others will be the envy of, as for a lot of companies to actually get paid when they have done the work would be heaven for them as they will often have to offer 30 days' credit (whether they get paid within those 30 days is then a massive battle in itself!) never mind getting half the money 4 weeks in advance!

The Profitable Clinic - The Skin Repair Group

The above point is magnified even further if you're taking rebooking deposits for 8 or 12 weeks' time, we are now entering cash flow heaven...

Key Point

Get your free copy of The Skin Repair Group cash flow spreadsheet to help manage your businesses cash flow by visiting:

www.theprofitableclinic.co.uk/free-bonus-gifts.

Chapter 7

The Power of Focus!

If your clinic is full each and every day of the week, then this point doesn't apply to you, please skip to the next chapter.

However, if you're reading this book, I am guessing there is room for improvement for you and especially if you're new to owning a business. In fact, at the beginning or after only a short period of time in business, to have a full clinic is quite an achievement and requires great marketing, sales, service, results and aftercare! But this chapter is all about the best way to build yourself up to just that level.

I see so many business owners opening up new days in their diary before they have even filled others up, as they are so desperate to get any business in at all costs (also don't underestimate your customer's ability to smell your desperateness, more on this later). Well don't!

What you need to do is FOCUS! Yes, focus on set days each week that you are to fill your diary with, they don't have to be the same day each week, you can rotate over a fortnightly or monthly cycle. However, what they do need to be is FULL!

You need each day to be focussed, so that the days you are doing treatments, you are focussed on JUST doing treatments. The days you are then not doing treatments you are working on making your business better!

This may sound simple but please don't underestimate the importance of this. Flitting from one task to another, doesn't allow your time to focus and really get stuck into the task in hand and if anything, makes you start to have too many balls in the air, all trying to be juggled at once...

It doesn't matter, what you choose to do non-treatment days, whether it be marketing to bring in more enquiries, sales to convert those enquiries you already have, ways to improve the service you offer or providing amazing aftercare but what it does need to be is not working in the business, but on the business.

This stops you getting distracted, starting one thing and then having to stop as a client has come in for a treatment, then not finishing or worse forgetting you had even started the task etc.

It's this power of focus that will allow you to take your business to the next level.

You can then start to add extra treatment days as you fill up all the planned treatment days. Once you are full, you will need to take on more staff or just allow your waiting list to go from 2 weeks to 2 months, the choice is yours!

Key Point

Concentrate on one task at a time until it's finished. If you don't complete a task, you may as well have not started it in the first place!

focus on 1 task
2 days booking
1 day marketing
1 day after care
1 day off

Chapter 8

Why You <u>Shouldn't</u> Be Scared To Put Your Prices Up?

Out of all the chapters, if I were to bet on the action points to be least implemented from all chapters, it would be this one! Why because you're scared. You think that by putting your prices up, you will lose all your customers, well if your service and offering are that bad in the first place then you're right, you will do!

However, I have a funny feeling that they really like you, which is why after all, they keep coming back! And if they like you, that means others will as well, and that includes customers who don't even know about you yet...!

Too many people, are too worried about what others are doing and not worried enough about what they are doing! Don't fret if your competition is cheaper than you, there is a place in the market for everyone and do you really want to be the one at the bottom. If you're not sure, I'll tell you about being at the bottom:

- The cheapest gets the cheapest customers.

- The cheapest customers complain the most.

- Those who complain the most, in general are often not happy.

- Those who are not happy, blame others for their unhappiness.

- Those that are blaming others for their unhappiness are not going to be recommending you to their family, friends or colleagues. Just moaning about you to them!

Do you want to be at the bottom of the pile of earnings, whilst dealing with the most problems? This equates to poverty and misery. Do you want to be poor and unhappy?

If the answer is yes, then keep your prices where they are! If you want to be happy and wealthy, then put your prices up. It's that simple.

Oh wait, I just heard you say "but it's ok for where you are, but for my area it's different"!! If only I had a pound for everyone who has said that to me over the years...
That's what everyone says, it's the same old excuse from everyone! I don't buy it and you're only saying that to make yourself feel better and stay in your comfort zone.

The middle is a fair place to be but when times get tough people in the middle may still need to look for cheaper
alternatives however the rich are still rich, whether it's a recession or not!

You want to be aiming for the higher end of the market, now it's not simply a case of just putting your prices up and you will attract these higher paying customers, you need to offer quality and value. So as long as your service, your treatment, your results, your after care and the whole overall feeling of the service you provide is creating value to your clients, then they will pay and pay top whack, they will!

If you don't believe me, ask yourself why/how do Louis Vuitton hand bags sell for 20 times the price of a handbag at Zara, which can look equally as nice while probably at best is made to twice the standard and certainly nowhere near the 20 times price premium it carries? Zara don't provide the value to the customer that LV can and does, that service and ultimately the special feeling inside the owner gets when both purchasing and thereafter of owning such a handbag...

If you're still not convinced, let me put it into perspective for you, generally a 5% increase in prices will generally equate to a 40% increase in your net profits! Yes, I will say that again as this is big, **a 5% increase in prices will generally equate to a 40%**

increase in your net profits! How can it have this big an effect on profits, well it's simple as that 5% increase will all be net profit as the old price takes care of costs, so all pure profit. That simple.

Key Point
Put your prices up! You will be surprised how highly your customers value you and a 10% to 30% price will be accepted.

Chapter 9

How to Close an Enquiry?

This book is about creating the most finely tuned clinic possible! Now a typical situation to find yourself in following an incoming call from an enquiry is, you spend ages going through everything, from giving great examples of why this treatment would be fantastic for them, to the fact find and then to make sure they are suitable and safe to have the treatment.

Next comes the easy part, after all that hard work that's just been done - choosing the best date for them to come in. However, a lot of businesses will just go through everything and then say "Thanks, just let me know if there is anything else we can help you with, bye"!!!!

Stop….!!

There are two very simple things to change that 20 minute call from wasting your time and letting that person slip away with you not having secured a booking, to actually taking a booking there and then before they have even had chance to think about your competitors...

First, is you simply just need to ask for the business, which is easy however it's not about just asking for the business, it's how you ask for the business, so with a few simple changes in the way you phrase it, really makes a huge difference.

NEVER ask the client "when would you like to come in?" This will provide them will all sorts of dilemmas and extra stress on should I do it this day, or can mum have the children that day, to I am having a work night out this day.

Instead, you make it easy for them by giving them 3 dates. This works so well on a number of levels, it limits the amount of choice they have when making a decision i.e. making it easy for them, whilst also making it appear that whatever date they select is their choice and finally you get to pick when you want to do it. Everybody wins!

Humans like choice however when you give them too much choice, the mind struggles with such a large selection and the fear of "what if I make the wrong decision/choice" kicks in and then you will never get a decision. People are terrified of making "the wrong choice", so you'll just get a "I'll think about it" or "I need to check with my partner" which 90% of the time (However not always!) are just polite ways of saying NO.

This is a game changer, especially when you think about all the steps you have gone through to get here and how it can easily be lost at the last hurdle…

Key Point

Never ask when, **ALWAYS** ask would the (date 1), (date 2) or (date 3) work best for you?

Chapter 10

Are You a Headless Chicken? Less is More...

Have you ever been to a restaurant and seen a menu full of so much selection and choice spread over 3 or 4 different pages? Well what's the first thing that springs to mind (other than the fact how can they keep all the products required to service this menu in stock and fresh!), it's tough deciding what you want from the menu as there is about 10 different things that take your fancy!

The same can happen with your clinic when there is just so much choice, people feel overwhelmed and often treatments will overlap further confusing your clients.

Next it will be how can they become a specialist at each dish if they are spreading themselves too thinly!

I have already covered the point in the last chapter about offering customers too much choice and the detrimental effect it has on business but I will mention it again! Choice is good BUT too much choice is **BAD**!

So, in this case, "Less is More".

No business can survive by being a "one trick pony", I have tried this model with our clinics trying to be a specialist in Skin Micro Needling for example. It sounds good in theory and I was surprised it didn't work but unless you're in London or maybe other big cities such as Manchester or Birmingham, where you have the huge numbers of people combined with great wealth and even then I am not sure it would thrive (I certainly wouldn't recommend taking the gamble either but I could be wrong!).

Like most things in life, finding the balancing point is where success lies, not at the extremities (unless of course your margins are extremely high and you're servicing very wealthy clients) of offering too much or trying to be too niche!

Where this middle ground is exactly, is hard for me to say as it will need to be based on your location and the desires of what your customers want and demand. However, what I do know, is it needs to work for you, on the basis of what is the most profitable use of your time.

Exercise

Go through every treatment you offer and work out the following:

 How much do you charge?

 The cost (only direct costs e.g. products and not indirect like rent) of providing this treatment?

3. How long does it take you?
4. Work out from the above your gross profit? (revenue less direct costs)

5. Next work out your gross profit per hour from this treatment? (how many treatments you can do in an hour multiplied by the gross profit you make or if it takes longer than an hour e.g. 2 hours divide the gross profit by 2 to break it back to an hour).

6. Do you enjoy it?

I have added the "Do you enjoy it" question as I am a big believer in your need to enjoy what you do! You spend a lot of your life working (not sure I like that name as it implies a hardship and not a passion or an enjoyable way to spend one's time). And I can think of far more lucrative industries I could be in, having had many opportunities to profit from them in the past and am sure many more such opportunities will present themselves in the future, however they don't interest me!

I am sure for a lot of you, this will also be the case! So make sure you do what you enjoy, while also making sure it makes you money. You can have both and don't ever be ashamed of having both as if you are creating value, it will come...

Once you have worked out the most profitable treatments that you offer, you can then begin focusing on what's the most profitable use of your time! If for example High Intensity Focused Ultrasound (HIFU) was the most profitable treatment for you, I know it is for us! Make sure you spend most of your marketing budget on HIFU, make sure you prioritise enquiries for HIFU, make sure your HIFU customers get the best service etc.

Then you keep working your way down the list of the most highly profitable (and enjoyable) treatments, so for us this would be fat freezing, so we again then put all our marketing budget we have left over from HIFU into Fat Freezing and these enquiries will be second on our list to call first!

Key Points

✓ Less is more! Offer a tempting range of treatments but don't over do it!

✓ Work out your most profitable treatments and focus on them!

Chapter 11

If at first you don't succeed, try, try, try again...

When clinics, Spas and salons are quiet most people resort to more advertising, now I wholeheartedly agree that this is important, but what about all those past enquiries...

Yes, what about all those past enquiries indeed! You are sitting on a gold mine and not doing anything about it...

Your best chance of booking a treatment in, is from your first call, which I am sure you are all more than aware of. Then with time, the chance of those enquiries converting decreases...

However, you can change this dynamic as a lot of people are still really keen even though their initial enthusiasm may have subdued as they have simply forgotten! So, by picking up the phone again you are reminding them of what they originally wanted.

But how many times should I be calling these people? What happens if I call too many times and piss them off?

The first thing to remember is that they got in touch with you, they gave you their details because they wanted something and NOT you trying to cold sell them something! That's really important to remember.

Next is that if you call a few times and they don't answer, then they may be genuinely busy and not ignoring you, this shouldn't come as a surprise to you as I am sure you're often too busy to take other people's calls as well!

Now, think about it from your perspective, how often have you enquired about something and each time the company has called and even though you have been too busy to take the call, you're glad they reminded you, as you had genuinely forgot all about this, even though this service/product is still of importance to you, well this is what also happens to your customers!

So don't just call these people back two or three times, this is not enough! I personally believe even five times is not enough, however this will still put you well ahead of the game.

Our general rule of thumb is, we will call someone up to 10 times, without a return of our voice message or missed call before we remove them from our call lists, if we have been a bit slack and not managed as many as 10 calls throughout the year, upon the anniversary of their enquiry we will remove them from our call lists.

What helps us is we have an email system that records all missed calls, this makes it easy to see the missed calls, you didn't even know you had missed! You can then record them in a spreadsheet or Customer Relationship Management (CRM) system and go about diarising the call backs.

This has proven highly effective for us, it allows you to really squeeze every last drop of juice out of your enquiries and also saves you a fortune on advertising.

Key Points

Can you see what calls you're missing, if not you need a phone system that can track calls.

Are you recording all of these missed calls on a CRM system or spreadsheet?

Are you calling all of your enquiries at least 10 times before giving up, or only once or twice?

Chapter 12

Overheads on Legs

What are these you may ask? Staff! Yes, those things that turn up for work late, forget to cross sell, moan and complain...

Ok so I am being a bit harsh in relation to some people (even if a very accurate description of a lot of staff, we've all had them!). I still can't believe the number of clinics, spa's and salons that don't have a full diary yet have staff standing around being idle, chatting to each other or more common with the invention of the smart phone, staff stood around texting, facebooking or whatever else they do with this personal computer glued to their hand continuously!

If you are not fully booked for 3 to 4 weeks in advance, then you have at least one member of staff too many!

The feeling of being booked up for a few weeks in advance is amazing, you have your next few weeks' cash flow already in the bank (as you have taken 50% deposits), combined with the fact you then know the amount of cash that will hit your bank account in the next 4 weeks.

This in turn allows you to plan business and personal expenditure more consistently and arguably the best fact of all, you are not constantly worrying about filling today/tomorrows empty slot and this overall feeling gives you an amazing inner confidence.

This inner confidence that now radiates from you, is very powerful and customers will pick up on it and in fact make your clinic, spa or salon even more desirable!

Plus, people often want what they can't have, so if they know you're full for the next month, they will want you even more now. I think I am feeling a "price increase" moment here...

The less worry you have, the more enjoyable your life will be and the more others will want to use you and be around you. So before taking on that new member of staff, ask yourself do you really need them or should we increase our waiting list to a few weeks instead of just the current one week.

I recall a Day Spa in South Wales, which was turning over around £8,000 per month yet had 8 staff! I could never quite get the maths on this one, as the building was fitted out to an excellent standard, rent/rates/bills were a few thousand a month and of course we haven't even touched on marketing or products! Yet for years the 8 staff stuck around, often just chatting for hours on the front desk. I don't think it's a surprise what happened to the business eventually but what was a surprise to me, was just how long it took for this to happen to the business...

While we are talking about staff, it's often surprised me how little importance clinics place on the first person who answers the phone! This is your first opportunity to WOW someone, we cover this in more detail elsewhere in the book however I just like to hammer home this point as it's your first chance to make a first impression!

Marketing and sales are key to a clinic's success, so rather than hire new aestheticians, why not recruit a sales person, if worried about the extra cost, you can also pay a lower basic and high commissions...

Key Points

Staff are often the most expensive cost of a business, so recruit carefully and wisely.

Before taking on extra staff have you thought about increasing your waiting list from 1 week to 4 weeks, then and only then take on your new aesthetician.

Why not take on a new sales person to bring in business before taking on a new person to do the business.

Chapter 13

Video Killed the Radio Star

Aside from being the title of a song I really like, it's true! Who advertises on radio these days? I am sure it can still be effective (I haven't ever tried but have looked into it) but it's just not COST effective! That's the key difference, radio will bring you customers but there are so many better and more efficient ways of doing so.

The key here is **VALUE** and return on investment!

When we first introduced videos of both our treatments and our of delighted customers, for the clinic and training side of the business we noticed a huge increase in conversion of enquiries and, I hate to admit this, but it took us a few weeks, maybe even months to realise what was driving this!

Then one day I said suddenly out loud, it's the videos! And so it was, what a cost effective form of advertising. A lot of the time, these cost us nothing to produce because they were free customer reviews we filmed at the end of a training because our clients were so delighted.

We have however used the services of a very talented video specialist called Jon Farley based in Bristol - his website is www.jonfarley.co.uk he has done all of our professional videos and some of the customer reviews however I do still like the authenticity of spur of the moment ones taken on the day, using just our phones which are more than adequate for the task in hand.

Videos serve a few different purposes, first off, we have them on our website so that people can see for themselves what it is we do, who we are and whether what we offer is for them. This also happens to save you hours on the phone as people can see for themselves both visually and in audio rather than just being another voice on the end of the phone.

The videos however make it more likely people will actually pick up the phone, and phone us they do in great numbers! Whats even better, is that it's a much easier conversion because they already know much more about us plus what to expect from the treatments.

So I am sure you can clearly see what a great form of marketing videos are. However, it doesn't stop there...

You can also put these videos on youtube.com and if they become popular enough they may even start to get shared which will in fact drive traffic to your website, all for free! Amazing isn't it?

But why stop at just youtube, put these videos on social media, send them out in emails to your customers both new and old and I am sure there are plenty of other ways that I haven't even thought of that they can be used for.

Quite a few clinics we've trained have already adapted this fantastic principle, so if you don't want to just take our word for it, take theirs too!

Key Points

Get yourself lots of videos showing who you are, some of the treatments you offer, frequently asked questions that your customers ask about your treatments and lots of customer reviews.

Once you have videos make sure you use them, so put them on your website, youtube and social media.

Videos of Rx
FAQ
Customer Reviews

Chapter 14

Website's the Basics

I did say this wasn't going to be a marketing book yet the last chapter talks about videos as part of your marketing offering, and now I am about to talk to you about websites again from a marketing perspective, however I make no apologies for this as these things are important and in fact very, very important.

Rather than me go on in detail how certain things on a website are very important to your success, I will keep it short and sweet. So without further ado, when designing a website you need to make sure the following apply:

1. **What's the Purpose – It Just Can't Be A Brochure**
   a. Are you selling something?
   b. Do you want visitors to call you?
   c. Do you want visitors to give you their contact details?

2. **The 10 Second Rule**
   a. The first fold has to grab their attention.
   b. Then persuade your visitors to stay longer.
   c. Is the site interesting/relevant for them?
   d. Is it for me?

3. <u>Google Analytics</u>

    a.   Consider what browsers people are viewing your site with and check it works well for all those browsers.

    b.   Is your website mobile responsive? Most people view websites on their phone now!

3. <u>Navigation Matters</u>

    a.   Don't be original or fancy.

    b.   Keep it consistent.

    c.   Don't put navigation above your logo.

4. <u>What Our Customers Say</u>

    a.   Separate page – with that heading.

    b.   Customer reviews interspersed throughout the site – every page should have a relevant one. Interwoven into the page.

    c.   Can't just be one liners.

    d.   Photos make a big difference.

    e.   Must include full names and location (try and use suburb if you just operate in one city/town)

5. <u>Make it Personal – People Buy People, Remember!</u>

    a.   Show nice photos of you and your team.

    b.   Show nice photos of your premises.

    c.   Use first names...a lot!

6. **Phone Number**
    a. Top right hand corner.
    b. Every page.

7. **Language**
    a. Use Friendly language.
    b. Engaging – Talk about your customer e.g. You not we! Twice as many You's as We's if 3 or 4 times more, even better!!!

8. **Images**
    a. Avoid stock photography – unless its highly original.
    b. No staged business shots.

9. **Video**
    a. Auto-play.
    b. Host on You Tube.
    c. Real and authentic – doesn't have to be slick and professional.
    d. 60-90 seconds is perfect.

10. **Home Page Critical Elements**
    a. Headline.
        i. Top Centre, Larger Font.

ii. Focused on "YOU" the customer, not "we" the business.

iii. Explain how you're going to:
- Make their lives easier.
-Save them money.
-Save them time.
-Entertain them.
-Make them more attractive.
- Help them feel better.

b. Opt in Offer

I. Avoid Newsletters as they just don't interest people and are ineffective.

II. Offer something of real interest, relevance and value to them.

III. The less you ask, the more enquiry forms you get filled out.

c. Direction to Action

I. Don't leave it to your navigation, add arrows and make it flow easily.

II. Be crystal clear why they should contact you.

III. Use graphics and tell them what you want to do e.g. call us and add the right level or prominence, so people notice.

    d. Good wording on your links for example which is better:
- I. "About Us" or "Discover Why Over 20,000 Business Owners Trust Us".
- II. "Products" or "Click here to find the best tools for your job"
- III. Plus embed links within the text.

However, it's also noting the things NOT TO DO while we are telling you what to do!

7 Common Mistakes

1. Too much colour, too many fonts, too busy.

2. Amateurish design and poor use of fonts.

3. Out of date content.

4. Slow loading graphics.

5. Not enough links in the text.

6. No differentiation – you're just like everyone else.

7. Poor site build so it looks bad on different browsers and screen sizes.

Key Points

You need to have a website.

If you have a website, it's worth investing the money in a good quality website or don't bother. Take great care in who builds your website as they will have a big impact on your business.

Chapter 15

Knowing Who your Customers Are?

Do you just take anyone who wants to pay you money? Do you even know who your ideal customer would be?

These are important, in fact critical questions you need to answer before you can even begin to target the right customers for you!

This relates back again to focus, in fact a lot of these business actions plans (chapters) are interrelated and feed off one another to create a stronger more profitable business.

The questions you should be asking yourself, is describe your perfect customer:

1. **Who are they – The Top 3?**

2. **Their Interests/Aspirations?**

3. **Who are you competing against for their money?**

4. **Their Role Models?**

The Profitable Clinic - The Skin Repair Group

To help you here is one I did a few years ago:

Who are they – Top 3?

Female 45 to 65 – Married, Older children, Husband high earner, starting to get concerned about age and looks, having more free time and money to do things they want.

Female 35 to 45 - Married & Single, Mothers, High Earners, Directors, Partners, Business Owners, Consultants, House Wives, Live locally, Competitive among peers.

Male 35 to 50 - Married & Single, Fathers, High Earners Directors, Partners, Business Owners, Consultants, Live locally, competitive.

Interests/Aspirations

Female 45 to 65 – Looking ones best, staying young, healthy lifestyles, House prices, interior design, horses, food, dinner parties, children's senior education, shopping, retirement planning, holidays, catching up with friends, career, child care, wine

Female 35 to 45 - Looking ones best, staying young, healthy lifestyles, House prices, interior design, horses, food, dinner parties, children's junior education, shopping, holidays, babies, dating, exercise/gym, catching up with friends, career, child care, wine

Male 35 to 50 – Cars, women, career, houses, drinking, rugby, football, cricket, gym, golf, holidays, children's education, DIY/Project managing interior design

Competition for Our Services

Female 45 to 65 – Second homes, education fees, holidays, clothes, handbags, home improvements, repairs, weekends away, facelifts, injectibles, Laser rejuvenation, detox retreats, pensions

Female 35 to 45 – Saving up for next house move, school fees, holidays, clothes/handbags, improvements/repairs, weekends away, Laser rejuvenation, tummy tucks, boob jobs, detox retreats, gym memberships, school fees

Male 35 to 50 – Cars, house purchases, TV & Electrical, holidays, suits, sporting equipment, school fees, home improvements/repairs, hair transplant.

Role Models

Female 45 to 65 – Madonna, Elizabeth Taylor, Audrey Hepburn, Michelle Pfeiffer, Helen Mirren.

Female 35 to 45 - Kate Winslet, Kate Moss, Victoria Beckham, Cameron Diaz.

Male 35 to 50 – David Beckham, Brad Pitt, Steve McQueen, Daniel Craig, Christian Bale, George Clooney

Then I would look to go a lot deeper once you have the overall and general feel for your desired customers by asking the below questions:

answer in your company (handwritten note)

1. What keeps them awake at night?

2. What are they afraid of?

3. What are they angry about? Who are they angry at?

4. What are their top 3 daily frustrations?

5. What trends are occurring and will occur in their businesses or lives?

6. What do they secretly, ardently desire most?

7. Is there a built in bias to the way they make decisions e.g. engineers = exceptionally analytical?

8. Do they have their own language?

9. Who else is selling something similar to your product and how?

The Profitable Clinic - The Skin Repair Group

10. Who else has tried selling them something similar and how has that effort failed?

Once you can answer these fully and have built up a profile of your perfect customers, it makes life a lot easier with your marketing, as you know who to target and make the advert more appealing for them and just them. Equally as important you now know where to target, saving you a fortune on your advertising spend as you are no longer spending your marketing budget in places that won't reach your target audience!

I believe this is called a WIN, WIN...

Key Points

✓Decide who your perfect customer is.

✓Describe in full the makeup of your perfect client.

✓Design all marketing and communication with this person in mind from here on in.

71

Chapter 16

Keeping Track of Your Customers!

Do you have a record of every individual customer you have ever had?

If not, I hope you've got a very good reason like "your clinic burnt down" or "your dog ate them all" as to why this is not already in place!

I will keep this chapter very much to the point. You need to have a record of every customer that pays you money.

You can have this in paper form if you really need to however as I have previously mentioned before a CRM system like Infusionsoft is invaluable and makes a very worthwhile addition to your team.

There are lots of very capable CRM systems out there but having researched the market back in 2013, Infusionsoft stood head and shoulders above the crowd, the market place would have changed significantly by now (2020) and whether Infusionsoft is still top of the pile, I am not sure but what I am sure of, is that Infusionsoft still delivers what it needs to in a very good way i.e. looking elsewhere would not be a good use of one's time.

One way to sum it up is this, Infusionsoft is like having an extra member of staff, it's that powerful, however be warned to learn Infusionsoft is a very time consuming process, I went on a 3-day course initially followed by another few days a week later!

It also doesn't stop there after a few days of training, you then have to implement everything you have learnt and boy does this take time and I mean TIME!

If you are looking for an excellent company to help with Infusionsoft or a CRM system in general, then I highly recommend Jumpworks in the midlands. We have used them for sometime, they are very knowledgeable and also importantly they are really nice as well, for more information visit their website www.jumpworks.co.uk.

Ironically, what I like about Infusionsoft is it has so many barriers to it being fully implemented, meaning most people won't bother to go to this much effort, which in turns means because you have, you now have a significant advantage over the competition!

I am not an expert on profiting from database customer lists, so I will keep it short as you can seek advice from more resourceful places however I do know that an up-to-date database working well can lead to fantastic re-occurring income from your existing client base, with very little effort.

The Profitable Clinic - The Skin Repair Group

Key Points

You need to record every single person who has ever paid you money for your services.

The system you use to record every customer needs to be user friendly as it's no good having all these records if you can't do anything with them!

53 Gloucester
road
RG30 2TH

Chapter 17

Those Little Extras

People love little extras, I liken it to you buy your children a fancy and expensive present and all they want to do is play with the box!

You have offered them cutting edge treatments expertly carried out, yet little things (that they've not come in for) such as offering them a drink upon arrival goes down extremely well!

Or perhaps when it's their birthday a £6 bottle of Prosecco with £5 chocolates will go down amazingly, well beyond your imagination!!

How do we know, because we do it! The little things are so important we should really be calling them the "little big things".

My main objective for this book, is it to become a working document for you, to write over, fold the corner of pages over, underline things etc. Plus, generally make it as easy as possible for you to implement everything in this book.

So, I have a put together a list of the "little big things" for you to implement today!

Here goes:

1. Return all calls within 24 hours - people don't like to think they have been forgotten about as it makes them feel unimportant.

2. When greeting customers always smile and show a genuine warm interest in them, let them talk about themselves and NOT you talking about yourself (as they don't care about you!)

3. Offer to take their coat.

4. Upon arrival offer all clients a drink, however be mindful of what drinks you are offering them and what values you want to be projecting eg offering them a double whisky on the rocks when they are coming in for anti-aging treatments!

5. Provide interesting reading material, relevant to your target audience so that they are entertained while waiting.

6. A comprehensive array of cushions and or pillows to provide the best level of comfort and support for your customers when on the treatment couch.

7. Charge extra for your treatments and then offer "complimentary" high quality cream or serum with every treatment, people love this. You can in fact go one step further and create a goody bag with things along the lines of nail polish, exfoliator, makeup, cleanser etc. This will make YOU the talk of the town as people will be totally WOWed!

8. Appointment cards (as you have already booked them back in for their next treatment), this helps remind them and also reminds them of you plus people like being given things!

9. If you have the man power, calling people up the next few days to see how they are getting on goes down really well, however this can be a job in itself, so make sure everything else is in line before doing this as some people will keep you on the phone for 30 to 60 mins! You have been warned.

10. For repeat customers, I would setup alerts (in your CRM) 2 weeks before it's their birthday and send them out a really nice birthday voucher with a monetary amount off, NOT a % off eg 10%! It needs to be actual money so they appreciate it more.

However, I wouldn't stop there, for those whose birthdays fall within 2 weeks either side of their treatment with you, I would give them 2 out of the following, a bottle of Prosecco (normal 750ml size please, we're not cheap or penny pinching!), box of tasty well-presented chocolates and/or flowers (don't have to be expensive, just look nice e.g. Tesco's £6/7).

11. Christmas, for those having treatments around Christmas time I would create two tiers, I would have low value presents i.e. under £10 for all customers who've spent over £100 with you that year.

Then for the big spenders, really go to town! We gave one lady who has had over 25 skin micro needling treatments with us (think it might even be 30 now), a free HIFU treatment last Christmas worth £2,000 and she loved it while also getting a great result!

12. I also believe having a "happy place" is great for your customers and helps put them in a great mood when they leave. Get rid of any staff who moan, are miserable or generally negative as they will be sending your customers elsewhere, making you miserable having to deal with them in the first place while simultaneously making you poor!

The above list even though very effective is not an exhaustive list and I am sure there are many other ideas that you have come up with over the years that will complement those.

To help you further, we have put together a clear and precise checklist of the "little big things" into an actionable format to make it as easy as possible for you to get the basics implemented and implemented now.

If you would like to download a free easy to use version of this for your clinic then please simply visit: www.theprofitableclinic.co.uk/free-bonus-gifts.

Key Points

The small things often are the big things!

Reward your Best Customers - they deserve it, they make your job fun, enjoyable and easy!

Chapter 18

First Impressions Really DO Count!

"You never get a second chance, to make a first impression"

In fact, I would add to this in your line of business, if you don't make a good first impression, you will never see that potential customer again! It's that straight forward. The good thing about first impressions is they are not that hard to create good ones...

Most people's first impression of you in today's world will be one of three things:

1. Your website (or social media pages).

2. Your premises.

3. Speaking with staff over the phone.

Let's start with your website and social media, I appreciate we have already covered this in a previous chapter however I find people learn better and are more likely to remember to do something when told of it multiple times, your website and social media need to be:

- Clean simple designs - No Clutter!

- Vibrant and positive colours.

- Good quality information and advice that helps your customers.

- Great quality photos of the excellent work you have done e.g. before and afters.

- Easy to contact you i.e. phone number in lots of different places so easy to find.

- A helpful feel to your digital platforms.

Your Premises, now this is probably the most simple to implement (and most boring), however has one of the biggest impacts and even more so if you have a busy frontage with lots of passing trade:

- CLEAN, yes absolutely bloody sparkling, EVERY DAY! Pay a cleaner an hour a day if your staff won't do it or you don't want to. The number of dirty clinics and salons I have been in never fails to amaze me.

- Tidy and clear of clutter, a similar ilk to above however this one is easier to spot as sometime with dirt you have to get up close to spot but with clutter it can hit you from miles away.

- Signage, do you have stupid fonts in fancy writing that no one can read, this annoys people! If they have an emotion of annoyance associated with you, they probably won't want to use you.

- External paint, is your paint peeling, tired looking and dull? If so, get the decorators in faster than you can say "it's like watching paint dry". Your frontage needs to be appealing and inviting.

- Your front entrance, as you are about to walk into any clinic the first thing staring at your customer for a few seconds before they enter your building is your door! Does it look amazing? Clean? With a high level of finish?

- Window and advertising displays, are they inviting? Do they create intrigue? Does it make your potential customers want to walk in to find out more? Are they clear and easy to read?

- Waiting area/reception is this a friendly and comfortable place to be? Good looking chairs, which are very <u>comfortable</u>.

- What's the atmosphere like? Is it like a doctors waiting room, with that ghastly cold silence? Your customers will hate this! Have happy warm music in the background to create a nice atmosphere, staffs aura is also key to this feeling.

- Internal decoration, are colours appealing to your desired customers? Is the paint bright and cut into a high standard with no marks to the walls? Are door frames and skirting boards finished to a high standard? All this is a reflection of you whether good or bad!

- Toilets, women love fresh clean toilets and as most of your customers will be women, you HAVE to get this right! Luxury loo rolls, beautiful smelling hand washes in high quality containers, fresh smelling fragrances, thick high quality paper towels or thick Egyptian cotton hand towels, big mirrors, something interesting to read facing your customers when sat on the loo (most likely the back of door!). I am sure there's more but you get the feel...

- Do you have cheap posters all over the clinic walls or have you had them framed to give a higher quality feel, as opposed to that poster curling over where the cello tape or blue tack has lost its adhesive!

Finally, customers first point of contact with you, will generally be speaking with staff over the phone. So this needs to be extra special:

- You need a friendly and helpful hello, with a what can we do for you attitude.

- Answer the phone in under 5 rings so that people aren't fed up waiting on the other end of the phone (this I appreciate can't be done all of the time).

Key Points

All of the above!

Chapter 19

Attitude & Likeability

You can get everything absolutely perfect both business operations and treatment offering but without the right attitude you may as well pour petrol over your premises and throw a match at it!

You're might be thinking to yourself, but my attitude is amazing, this is all I ever wanted to do and one of the reasons I am reading this book is that I am enthusiastically trying to improve my business to be the best. You however are unlikely to be the problem!

How your staff are to your face can be completely different to how they are to each other and more importantly to your customers. A massive warning is a staff member who can't even be bothered to hide their bad attitude when communicating with you, I dread to think what they will be like with your customers and other staff!

Consumers don't think to themselves, oh that member of staff's attitude is terrible but she's probably just having a bad day or that it's only her that's bad. NO, they will brandish the whole business as having a bad attitude and won't want to spend their money with you again.

Attitude is so important and arguably the most important aspect of a successful business. In fact, when recruiting, make a point of recruiting for attitude as most skills can be learnt easily with time but attitude is very difficult to be taught, someone either has it or they don't.

If a staff member has a bad attitude, they won't just be losing you customers for good, they will be infecting other members of staff who up to now have been assets to your business. In time their negative bad ways will slowly erode at all but the best people, creating a toxic business which may never recover from having employed such cancerous people.

On the flipside of this, if your staff have a great attitude, then sales will seem to appear if like magic from nowhere! Your customers will love dealing with your clinic, they will look forward to coming in next and they will have such a positive feeling towards your business that sales will become easy.

Key Points

Attitude generally is not something that can be taught, someone either has it or they don't. If they don't have it from the start, don't ever entertain taking that person on or it could be the single most worst decision as a business owner you ever make.

Chapter 20

Selling Up - I'm Out of Here!

Ever worry about how you're going to sell your business and release the huge amount of value tied up in your business?

Your Exit Strategy - As You Might Never Know When It's Time to Leave...

Do you want to be doing what you're doing now, forever? Of course, not! Us humans always need fresh and new challenges to keep us stimulated and fulfilled, right?

The other main reason why you would want to sell your business is retirement. Very rarely do people want to sell their business just because they want money. When they decide they want out, of course they want the money for their business but very rare is the money in itself the driver of why they want out.

This leads us to the two main reasons, boredom and retirement. Personally, I love what I do now but am aware I don't want to be doing this all my life as lots of other great things I want to experience and do both in this industry and others.

I know that I may want to sell my business in the next 10 years and putting the right systems, procedures in place combined with speaking to the right people now, means that when the time is right, I am in a position to leave, when I want to leave.

Importantly, not leave it down to other people to create my exit strategy for me, on their terms.

What are you going to do with your aesthetic business when the time comes for you to move onto the next stage in your life? I bet your thinking, that's easy, I'll just sell it!

Well, have you ever sold a business before? It's certainly not like selling a house, whereby you ring up an agent, give it a lick of paint, a few viewings, maybe the odd sale that falls through before it finally completes, but all in all, relatively plane sailing.

Are you aware what might be very precious to you and has provided you with a great lifestyle for many years, might not be so appealing to others?

In this chapter I want to briefly cover the below aspects:

1. Your different options of how to sell your business.
2. Advantages of all the different options.
3. Disadvantages of all the different options.

4. Helping to fund your buyer and creative financing solutions.
5. How to still maintain control of your business until they have fully paid you, if offering a part payment sale.
6. Who are the likely people to buy your business?
7. If you can't sell, how to create the systems & controls, that allow you to keep your business and income with little day to day management.

The time when you want to leave this exciting industry your currently thoroughly enjoying, may seem a million miles away today, however, as I am sure you can relate to, the older you become, the quicker time seems to just vanish into thin air!

Those weeks turn into months and years race by, and before you know it you could be needing to retire soon or have a list of things you want to achieve while you still can. This means your current business is surplus to requirements.

The most important thing to take from this checklist is NOW is the time to be planning your exit. Not next week, not next year but now! The majority of people reading this book won't however plan this now, as they think there are more important things to do and it can wait, but as we all know, time waits for no one...

Let's start with the issues you will face when coming to sell your business?

The Questions You Need to Ask Yourself, Before You Begin the Sale Process?

Selling your business is a significant point in your life and before you rush into it, you need to step back and have a think, preferably while away for a few days or even a week so that you have a clear mind, in a relaxed environment without the pressure of work clouding your judgement!

Ask yourself:

1. How much money do you need to live off, whether this is for retirement (don't forget to add in pensions), a gap year or just a few years out to decide what you want to do and have the time to set it up?

2. What do you want to achieve as a sale figure?

3. Can the business support this valuation now?

4. If not? What are you going to do so it can in a few years?

5. What else in life do you want to achieve?

6. When would you like to do this?
7. Who am I going to target to sell the business to?

8. What systems and processes do I need to put in place now in order to sell my business?

9. Or can you put the systems in place so that the business provides you with an income when you are no longer working in the business as an alternative to selling?

Like most things, there is no right answer, some will work better for others but knowing your options will help to increase the chance of you getting the exit you want.

Your Options of How to Exit Your Business.

1. What Happens to Most People's Businesses? They just simply close down and walk away with nothing for the last 10 to 30 years of their lives work! This is the easiest option however doesn't give you much financial freedom in your retirement.

2. There are so many businesses that have been going for 20 years, that are turning over millions of pounds, have great clients, great staff but if the owner can't sell or it can't run without their involvement, they ultimately fade away...

3. Trade Sales, this is great if you're looking for an escape, then you might be able to structure the sale of your business in terms of a clean exit (therefore no ties or further commitments expected of you) but typically if you're looking for a clean exit, you'll get a lot less value for your company than if you're prepared to do earn outs.

4. Earn Outs, the challenge is that if you've reached a point in your life where you're sure you want to sell your business, then continuing to work in your business for the next 3 to 5 years as an employee of somebody else, is a pretty disheartening way to exist.

5. What often happens in the earn out scenario is that they sell their business on a trade 5 year earn out, but they rarely last a year because even though they're theoretically in charge of their business, they no longer have full authority. They have the responsibility to continue to grow their business to hit targets but now they must go and request budget in order to grow the team to achieve it. All the joy has been sucked away...

6. Your approached by a competitor, this does happen and is probably the best strategy as little work for you both sourcing buyers and getting the business sale ready, no agents' commissions and as they have approached you, they are genuinely willing and able

to pay you the most for your business. These however are extremely rare.

7. Mergers and Acquisitions, companies getting together to create a combined business just bigger. Now this might sound like something you read in The Financial Times or watch on business news and think I can't do this! Well, yes you can. It's a lot simpler than the "professional advisors" make out. I understand why, as they are in a position to profit heavily from your company in both fees and commissions.

Getting Your Business Ready to Sell, For When You Want to Sell...

I have put together a comprehensive checklist list of all the aspects you need to ensure are completed, up-to-date and clearly documented in order for you to get the best price possible for your business.

If you would like this then please visit:
www.theprofitableclinic.co.uk/free-bonus-gifts

Who's Going to Buy Your Business?

The trade sale route, you need to be prepared to do a lot of your own research to find out who will buy your business. Below is a good starting point however it's certainly not an exhaustive one:

- Competing clinics both locally and nationally who are looking to increase their presence in your area.

- Equipment suppliers, having their own clinic without the hassle and cost of setup make showcasing their products in a real life setting, a lot more appealing to potential customers. Same goes for fellow equipment suppliers offering different products, they can make for great business purchases.

- Doctors and nurses, how many of us know doctors/nurses who have had enough of the NHS and would love to open their own Aesthetic Practice, putting their valuable skills to use, but perhaps just don't know how! Well, they do now, as they can buy yours in 3 to 5 years' time when they are looking to leave.

- Listing websites, they can be cheap and effective but very much dependant on others who happen to be searching at that particular time and knowing what they want, as opposed to giving people ideas who didn't know they fancied owning a clinic!

- Product suppliers, who for the same reasons as equipment suppliers want to showcase their products in a clinic environment.

- Finally, don't write off friends or acquaintances as often people are looking for a new challenge and don't quite know what, plus everyone (I know from personal experience when socialising) loves the aesthetics industry and they spend most of the night chewing your ear off in the search of forever lasting youth!

Who's Going to Pay for All This?

Last and arguably most importantly, how are they going to pay for your business?

I know as a 12 year old boy, I was Ferrari and Lamborghini's most enthusiastic buyer, just one huge problem my £12 a week paper round wasn't going to help much to buy a £100,000 Ferrari Testarossa!

Banks will lend against business acquisitions but the company needs to have 3 years' accounts, all saying the right thing and it might be that you've only got the company in order in the last 18 months, which doesn't help your value or the purchasers request of finance.

Re-mortgaging the purchaser's homes is a good one especially for those in the South East and hot spots like Bristol, where a £200,000 home has quickly become a £600,000.

Or you can finance the purchase for them! Now I appreciate this sounds absurd as it's you who wants money from them and not the other way around.

They pay you an upfront lump sum, say 10% and then the balance every month or quarter. You then take a charge/debenture over the company and if they fail to make payment, you simply take the company back and sell it all over again. Plus this time you've now got the experience of selling a business, you never know maybe the losing bidders still want your business?

Here is an example:

Your profits are £100,000 (that's what you take out of the business plus retained earnings for future investments in the business e.g. renovations, new staff, new devices etc).

Sale Multiple of 3 times profits or earnings.

Sale price £100,000 x 3 = £300,000

10% Upfront payment from buyer of your business = £30,000

Remaining balance of £270,000 paid over 5 years.

£4,500 per month from buyer of your business for 60 months.

The Profitable Clinic - The Skin Repair Group

Key Point

You need to plan now, yes today, in order to get the exit price and time right for your lifestyle as if you wait until you want to sell it, it will already be too late.

For further help on selling your business please visit: www.theprofitableclinic.co.uk/free-bonus-gifts

Part 2 - Your New Offering

Chapter 21

What Treatments Will Make My Clinic Profitable?

I had intended this to be the last chapter of the book before the summary however a few of our clients when reading the draft version of the book suggested that it could be further improved by going into more detail on the more profitable treatments, rather than just listing them in this chapter and say off you go and do your own research, which of course we still recommend you do...

The treatments are as follows:

1. Skin Micro Needling.
2. High Intensity Focused Ultrasound (HIFU).
3. Cryotherapy Chambers.
4. Fat Freezing.
5. Injectables - Anti-wrinkle and Filler.
6. The Oxygen Facial
7. Hyperbaric Oxygen Therapy (HBOT).
8. HIFEM Accelerated Muscle Stimulation.

Before we go into detail on those excellent value adding treatments, I want to discuss why this is important to your business.

First off is the realisation that you are a time based business, I appreciate you can get more locations, more staff, more treatment rooms, but what you do have is clear cut limits unlike say MasterCard, who make billions of transactions all over the world and probably every day not even per annum! We aren't in that almost limitless business and if honest nor would you want to be, as it's probably quite boring!

We have to take a very precious view when it comes to our time and what we get per hour for that time. This leads me to ask 1 question:

1. Are you offering low margin high volume treatments?

2. If so how much per annum NET profit do you make from each of these low margin treatments?

You should already know the answer to both of those questions but if you don't I would certainly go off and make the calculations, then work out:

1. Is it profitable?

2. If so is it worth the profit for the time, effort and hassle?

If the answer is No, then the following chapters will be music to your ears, as you will be able to not just get double or treble the amount of revenue per hour from your clinics time, but realistically 10 TIMES the amount!

I will repeat that again for those that thought that was a misprint, you can easily achieve 10 times the revenue from the treatments described in the following pages over the low margin treatments that you may be currently offering.

Having said that I do appreciate a lot of these low margin, high footfall treatments are great to pay the overheads and most importantly provide a huge client base in order to promote the more profitable treatments you offer. Please don't think this is lost on me. However, for some, this is lost on and that's what I want to make you aware of.

Before I provide a real life example, I want to uncover a common mistake too many clinics/salons make. They see the amount they are generating per hour in sales/revenue/turnover and think that's amazing, I am going to be rich, but they are not considering the gross profit per hour and even more importantly the NET PROFIT per hour. This is the money that at the end of the week, year, month hits your bank account. Very important.

A quick example of this is The Skin Repair Pen which is a micro needling device that's used to treat stretch marks, acne scarring, general scars and great for anti-ageing (I personally have it every 2 to 3 months and will continue to do so for the rest of my life!). This treatment retails from between £199 to £399 throughout our range of training clients nationwide in the UK.

If you're offering low margin treatments like massage, nails, microdermabrasion it doesn't take a genius to work out you're going to need to do between 5 and 10 times the number of microdermabrasion's just to generate the same revenue.

However, it doesn't stop here, I said generate the same amount of revenue NOT net profit. To service 10 microdermabrasion treatments, you will need to:

- Spend 10 times the amount on marketing - both time and money.

- You will need to spend 10 times the time on the phone booking them in.

- Actually find 10 clients.

- 10 times the amount of client admin and support.

- 5 to 6 more hours of staff time (micro-needling take about twice the time per treatment).

- 10 times the amount of treatment consumables.

I could go on but I'm sure you get the idea...

All of the above costs time, so even though you have had to spend 6 times the amount of time to get the same revenue, you in fact make a lot less profit!

Ultimately, we go into business for 2 things, we enjoy what we do and we want to make money in order to live good lives, so why not make the most out of your time!

I also have to say using that example, regardless of the fact that you're making more money, the example is great as you are providing your client with a much better service as the results they will get from micro needling will be far more significant than from microdermabrasion, which in turn will make them a happier client and then more likely to return and recommend you, even if this is going off my original point.

Key Points

Your time is limited and you need to ensure you offer treatments that increase your clinics per hour rate.

Understand the difference between revenue, gross profit and the most important one of them all, net profit. While we're on this topic I will remind you of the old saying...

"Turnover is vanity, Profit is Sanity and CASH is KING!"

Chapter 22

Your Complete Business Plan

Before we would advise on investing in any new profitable treatments to your clinic, we need to make sure you have the basics right first.

There is no point investing in great new treatments if your business is not being operated properly. It's like those couples who are having relationship problems and decide to have a baby to "make things better"!

You need solid foundations before you can even think of investing in any new treatments, no matter how profitable they are!

For this reason, I would like to cover the key aspects you need to have both planned and more importantly actioned.

Taking from our *"Tripe P Program"*, the world's most comprehensive marketing, sale and business program for clinic owners, we developed over the last decade to ensure our customers succeed, I've outlined the things you need to be aware of and actually be DOING.

How to Sell Treatments!

Over the years we have realised that even though our trained customers are excellent medical professionals and aestheticians, whether completely new to aesthetics or with years of experience, the one thing they never get taught is how to *"Sell Their Treatments"*.

We've broken back the key elements to make your clinic more profitable, they are:

1. Promote.
2. Profit.
3. Protect.

This framework is extremely comprehensive yet very easy to use, with each of *The Triple P's* further broken down into 19 modules/subjects each i.e 57 aspects of your business to review and improve, in total across all 3Ps.

This allows you to quickly and easily implement each key area without getting overwhelmed and generate new sales for your business. However, remember your ultimate aim is to make your clinic - PROFITABLE and not just increase sales!

P1 - Promote

Promote is the foundation of any business. Without promote, you don't have a business, you have a hobby!

For years people have talked about if you build it, they will come! Well this is absolute rubbish.

Below are the key elements that make up the Promote module, this serves as your solid foundations to ensure your clinic is getting the lifeblood it needs daily - Clients!

1. What the Ultimate Clinic or Salon looks like?

2. Problem Solving - That's What You Really Do!

3. Your Perfect Client?

4. What You Represent to The World?

5. Why Looks Matter - External Clinic Branding.

6. Websites that WOW.

7. Making Sure People Can Find You Online?

8. The Most Important Place to Be?

9. Paying for Clicks.

10. Video Killed The Radio Star.

11. Is Their Door Mat Naked?

12. Lost in Facebook.

13. A Picture Paints a Thousand Words - Instagram.

14. Keep in Touch While You Sleep - Email Automation.

15. Making it Real - Case Studies & Reviews.

16. Not Another Brochure - Consumer Buyer Guides.

17. Make Yourself Famous - Locally!

18. Your Clients Mouths are Full of Gold - Referrals.

19. Conversion Rate Optimisation (CRO)

P2 - Profit

Arguable my favourite module, this builds on the great momentum you have now built up with lots of new clients, however now that you have plenty of clients, before you go out and get more. STOP!

The Triple P philosophy is about making your clinic PROFITABLE and not about generating the biggest turnover, and for that reason, we look into the best ways to maximise the profits you generate from each client whilst providing the best value and service in the industry for your clients. It's all about value creation for you AND your clients!

Below are the key elements that make up the Profit module, this ensures your clinic is PROFITABLE!

1. Making the Most of What You Got - Profit Maximisation.

2. Goal Setting - Getting What you Want from Life?

3. Mindset is Everything.

4. The Power of Focus.

5. Sell Without Even Selling.

6. Your Business Numbers & Ratios.

7. Pricing for Profit.

8. Getting More from Less - Doubling Sales

9. The Profitable Menu.

10. Five-a-Side Covering Letters.

11. Recruiting Your Team.

12. JVs - Getting Others to Sell for You.

13. These Are Special People - VIP Clients.

14. Offer the Best - New Treatment Offerings.

15. Customer Relationship Management Software.

16. Now That's a Deal - Offers.

17. In Clinic Branding & Promotion.

18. Done for You - Your In-Clinic Decorators.

P3 - Protect

Then finally, you need to look at ways to protect you and your clinic from your competition as once they see how successful and busy you are, they will be wanting to COPY YOU!

It's for that reason you need to take protecting your business as a priority.

Below are the key elements that make up Protect, this serves as your team of security!

1. Why the Final P - Protect, Is So Important?

2. Your Wellness and High Performance.

3. Staff Motivation & Loyalty.

4. WOW Them - Customer Service.

5. Making Sure Clients Show Up.

6. Making Sure Your Clients Return.

7. Cash is KING.

8. A Photoshoot - You're the Star!

9. Get Yourself Listed Locally.

10. Keep Them Loyal.

11. Sacking Clients.

12. Texting to Profits.

13. It's Your Birthday (& Christmas).

14. Your Website Facts - Google Analytics.

15. Red Carpet Events.

16. Everybody's a Winner.

17. Winning Awards.

18. Get in Costume.

19. They Don't Need You Anymore - Systems & Processes.

20. I'm Out of Here - Selling Up.

If having gone through all the above key aspects to making your clinic profitable and you either haven't got those in place or don't feel like actioning them, here are a few questions to ask yourself.

- What will the twenties look like for Your Business? Your Family? Your Life Style?

- Do you want your business to be more successful this year than it was in last year?

- Would you like more holidays and nicer holidays?

- Do you want a new car, in fact a better car?

- Would you want to expand your business and take on more staff?

- Do you want to move and buy a bigger, nicer house in a better area for your kids to grow up in?

- Would you like to achieve financial freedom for you and your family?

If you would like more information or help putting together an industry leading business plan for your future success, then please visit:
www.theprofitableclinic.co.uk/triple-p-program.

Chapter 23

Skin Micro Needling

I've said for a long time now, that if I had to choose just one anti-ageing treatment for the rest of my life, it would have to be the one and only Skin Micro Needling using The Skin Repair Pen.

I personally have this treatment every 2 to 3 months due to the amazing radiance it gives my skin and the reduction in lines and wrinkles. However it doesn't just provide excellent anti-ageing solutions. It can help with:

- Anti-aging and wrinkle reduction.
- Tightening and thickening of the skin.
- Stretch Mark Removal.
- Acne Scar Removal.
- Hyper-pigmentation and Melasma.
- General Scaring.
- Cellulite.
- Hair Regeneration.
- And I am sure the wonders of this treatment will reveal more benefits over the years with its ever increasing popularity.

It works by creating thousands of micro injuries every minute piercing the skin with depths of between 0.2mm and 2.5mm, the depth of course varying on where on the body and/or face you're treating.

Traditionally the devices used to offer this treatment were rollers however they became obsolete about 6 to 7 years ago with the development of the Micro Needling Pens.

Popular Questions Asked About Skin Micro Needling

Is it safe?

Yes, if the appropriate health and safety checks beforehand are carried out thoroughly and the client is suitable for treatment.

Does it hurt?

No, we do recommend that you use topical anaesthetic, which are very effective when applied for the correct length of time.

How long does the treatment take?

You will need to allocate around 90 minutes to allow time for both the topical anaesthetic and the treatment itself, including post treatment aftercare.

How much can you charge for this treatment?

We recommend anywhere from £199 to £399 depending on the size of the area to be treated, your experience, the level of service you offer, if you provide skin care products and creams inclusive, your clinic location and market place.

How does it work?

After using The Skin Repair Pen, your body will start to naturally regenerate and repair the skin, working below the surface in the dermis. New collagen is formed, new skin cells are generated and blood supply is enhanced after the treatment, however it can take up to 6 weeks before visible signs of regeneration and repair are seen. Most people will see an improvement sooner than this.

How long does the treatment last?

The process will continue over the following months, providing you with a natural and long lasting enhancement. This is your own collagen, so there is no need to wait for a product to break down, meaning the repair is permanent until your body breaks down collagen as it naturally would through the ageing process.

How will my skin look?

Initially the skin could look red for around 24- 48 hours after the treatment, however for some people this could be less or it could be more depending on how sensitive your skin is.

The skin may become dry and tight shortly after the treatment, this is a completely normal reaction and we can provide specialist skin repair cream to help with this. After this, the skin will look brighter and more vibrant, then approximately six weeks later the regeneration and repair process starts to tighten the skin.

How many treatments will I need for rejuvenated skin?

The number of treatments required will depend on the condition of the skin or if for acne the type of acne scar and its severity. We recommend a course of 3 to 6 treatments as a minimum to achieve maximum results for more even and smoother looking skin.

Key Point

Business Packages start from just £1,495 for training and equipment for Skin Micro Needling, which makes it a very low barrier to entry to start offering this fantastic treatment.

This low investment combined with the fact you can charge up to £399 a treatment make this offering very lucrative for you. Plus not forgetting it can treat over 8 different types of popular concerns your clients will have.

Chapter 24

High Intensity Focused Ultrasound (HIFU)

Now if I could only choose two treatments to have for the rest of my life then HIFU or High Intensity Focused Ultrasound, would join the ranks of Skin Micro Needling. It also goes hand in hand with skin micro needling with both complimenting each other very well. And perhaps it's only because I am not old enough yet for gravity to have taken its full effects on my eyes, nasolabial lines, marionette lines, jowls, submental and neck area, that's it's second in my regular must have treatments to Skin Micro Needling.

However, I do believe if I wrote this book in 5 to 10 years' time, my thoughts would probably be putting HIFU over Skin Micro Needling, due to its incredible lifting effects on gravity inflicted faces!

Arguably, this procedure is your next best thing to an actual face lift. Obviously, not possible to get the exact same benefits from a surgical face lift, however this treatment gets as close as possible without a knife in sight. It wasn't that long ago that outside of London, very few places offered this cutting edge treatment. Luckily now for the UK population this is starting to change.

HIFU is literally what it says it is, high intensity focused **ultrasound**. We are sending this ultrasound energy into the skin focused at different depths dependant on where we are treating.

HIFU therapy lifts, tightens and tones lose skin to counteract the effects of both time and gravity. One of the first effects of gravity is that the brows descend and the eyes start to appear smaller. HIFU can lift the brow, which in turn reduces the excess skin on the eye lids, opens up the eyes and gives you a more refreshed, brighter and youthful appearance.

This treatment really comes into its own for:

• Lifting and sharpening the jowl area and jaw line (say goodbye to unwanted double chins and turkey necks!)

• Softening the nasolabial lines and lifting the cheek.

• Lifting the brow and reducing excess skin on upper eyelids.

• Tightening loose skin around the stomach from childbirth or weight loss.

• Tightening "bingo wings".

Where this treatment really excels is that it's a one-off treatment. However arguably, best of all there is no downtime with HIFU, so you can go back to work that very afternoon!

Popular Questions Asked About HIFU

What Makes This Treatment So Special?

HIFU is the only non-surgical skin rejuvenation procedure that can specifically target and strengthen the deep foundational layer of tissue that doctors address in surgery. The ability to treat not just the skin, but its underlying support, from the inside out, helps to ensure both safe and satisfying results, with no downtime.

Does it Hurt?

There can be some discomfort while the energy is being delivered, but it is temporary and a signal that the collagen-building process has been initiated. Comfort thresholds vary from client to client, and practitioners will discuss with clients options for making the experience as pleasant as possible. Clients typically leave comfortable and excited about the benefits to come.

What Can I Expect Afterwards?

Clients are able to return to their normal activities right away and there are no special measures needed.

Skin may appear a bit flushed immediately after the HIFU therapy, but any redness should disappear within a few hours. It is not uncommon to experience slight swelling or tingling/tenderness to the touch for a few days to weeks following the procedure, but these are mild and temporary in nature.

There is the possibility of other less common post-procedural effects, such as temporary small areas of bruising or numbness, which your practitioner will review with you.

Is HIFU Safe?

Ultrasound energy has a proven track record, with use in the field of medicine for over 50 years. Clinical trials have demonstrated the safety of this latest application.

What Kind of Results Can Be Expected?

With just one treatment, the regenerative process is initiated. But the full effect will build gradually over the course of 3 to 12 months. Some clients may benefit from more than one treatment.

Visible effects include a lifting and toning of loose skin. This results in reduced skin laxity on the eyelid and a more open, youthful look to the eyes overall. Clients have also reported firmer, better-fitting skin in other areas of the face and neck too.

There is also an invisible result from the procedure with the creation of new collagen, which gives the skin its youthfulness.

Who is a Good Candidate for HIFU?

A good candidate for HIFU is someone with skin that has "relaxed" to the point of looking, and often feeling, less firm. A lowered brow line or sagging skin on the eyelids, for instance, is often the first sign of "maturing" skin.

That being said, getting in early and using this treatment as a preventative measure to stop and reduce any signs of aging before they have set in, has given us fantastic results and very happy clients, this is because the skin still has a good level of laxity.

While it does not duplicate the results of surgery, HIFU therapy has proven to be an inviting alternative for those who are not ready for surgery.

How is HIFU Different to Laser Procedures?

HIFU uses sound energy, ultrasound, which has unique properties that allow it to bypass the surface of the skin to treat depths not matched by any other non-invasive cosmetic device. HIFU stimulates collagen production in the skin's foundation, resulting in a clinically significant lift of tissue over the following 2-3 months.

Lasers rely on light energy, which cannot reach deeper skin layers at an optimal temperature, so laser treatments typically only treat superficial skin. Since the two technologies often treat different types of skin issues, they're actually very compatible.

How Does HIFU Stimulate Collagen Production?

During the treatment, the transducer delivers and deposits focused ultrasound energy deep beneath the skin at the optimal temperature for collagen regeneration. The treatment jumpstarts a natural process, known as neo-collagenesis, to produce fresh, new collagen. The treatment itself doesn't involve any creams, fillers or toxins, it just relies on your body's own collagen-building process for natural, noticeable results.

How Long Does a HIFU Treatment Take?

The length of the treatment will depend on the area being treated and your individual treatment plan. A face and neck procedure typically takes 60-90 minutes, while a chest treatment on its own takes approximately 30 minutes.

Will You Need to Take Time Off Work?

With a single HIFU treatment there is no downtime. After your procedure, you can resume your normal activities immediately, without having to follow any special post-treatment measures. We have even had clients come in to the clinic on their lunchbreak to have the treatment, no creams required and your general skin care plan and make-up can be applied as normal.

How Many HIFU Treatments Will You Need?

Most clients only need one treatment. However this may be based on the degree of skin laxity, the biological response to ultrasound energy and the individual's collagen-building process, some clients may benefit from additional treatments. Because your skin continues to age, future touch-up treatments can help clients keep pace with the body's natural aging process.

How Much Does HIFU Cost?

The cost of an HIFU treatment can range widely depending upon the size of the area being treated. Prices start from £495 for one area and for a full face and neck at high end clinics expect to pay £5,000, especially if surgeon led.

Are There Any Side Effects?

The skin might appear flushed at first, this can mainly be during the treatment but sometimes lasting a little longer, the redness should however disappear within a few hours. Some clients experience slight swelling, tingling or tenderness to the touch, but these are temporary in nature.

Other, less common post-procedural effects may include temporary bruising or numbness on small areas of skin. As with any cosmetic procedure, there is the possibility of other rare side effects, which your practitioner will review with you.

How Long Does it Take to Notice Results and How Long do They Last?

After your HIFU Treatment, you may see an initial effect, but the ultimate results will take place over 2-3 months, as your body naturally regenerates collagen. Since the procedure stimulates your own collagen production, how long the results last really depends on you. The treatment produces new collagen on the inside, but your natural aging process will dictate how long that translates into visible results on the outside.

Key Point

A HIFU machine though a similar investment to most aesthetic equipment, provides greatly increased returns with most clinics charging between £495 and £1,995 for a full face and neck, for a treatment that takes around 90 minutes, this machine can seriously up your profitability.

Chapter 25

Cryotherapy

Cryotherapy which literally means "cold therapy" is a treatment where your body is exposed to temperatures of around -110°C to -180°C. The treatment takes as little as 2 to 3 minutes, but the effect on the body is most spectacular. The extreme cold provides stimulus that then activates physiological processes within the body.

It's effectively like a system reboot of your body, as the body scans itself for underperforming bodily functions and repairs itself rapidly. Although you can get improvements from just one session, to see the full benefits, one has to have around 10 treatments to fully experience the greatness of this treatment.

The range of use is varied, with the very best athletes in the world having up to 2 treatments a day when training intensively, and then to those just wanting the well being and health benefits having a course of 10 treatments daily, before dropping down to just a few treatments every month.

Even though the temperatures can go down to -180°C, it's surprising, as it doesn't actually feel that cold! Getting out of a warm bed in the middle of winter can feel much worse...

Why Have Cryotherapy?

Cryotherapy provides many and varied benefits, which is why such a diverse range of people swear by cryotherapy as their treatment of choice for a great life. Below are the main ones that come up, time and time again.

Faster Recovery

The main reason for this is the huge reduction in inflammation (the body's natural healing process) after having cryotherapy. Plus, the release into the blood stream of oxygen and hormones.

It also helps flush out harmful toxins from within the body. All in all, this allows you to return to training quicker and in turn train harder, to become even faster and stronger.

Faster Healing After an Injury

For the same reasons as above, you can heal much faster from an actual injury as well as just intensive training. It can also help to reduce the pain associated with an injury. Boxing, MMA and UFC professionals are all extensive users of cryotherapy and are very vocal about its benefits and advantages it's given them.

Other sports that may cause one to suffer from things such as repetitive strain injuries, such as tennis and golf, are also fast beginning to realise its benefits and the competitive advantage it gives them over their rivals.

However it's not just sports stars that benefit from injury recovery, anyone can! You will also experience less muscle spasms, fast and effective removal of excess heat from the point of injury, lymphatic drainage is drastically improved and finally for the same reasons as to why hyperbaric oxygen therapy is very effective, you are increasing the blood flow of oxygen rich blood cells again speeding up the recovery time.

Increased Immunity

Cryotherapy is fantastic for stimulating the body's immune system, via the improved production of hormones triggered by exposure to cold temperatures. This in turn increases your body's immunity to day to day infections and colds.

Enhanced Hormone Production

Though mentioned above the improvements in the body's production of hormones justifies its own section as it will increase testosterone production while reducing your stress hormones, a win, win! It doesn't stop there, as endorphin levels are also improved, which all help to reduce antioxidant stress within the body.

Sleep Recovery Insomnia

It helps to relax you while simultaneously reducing anxiety, which all lead to a better night's sleep. Also, it can make you tired, so this again helps you to sleep a lot easier and the quality of sleep is also improved.

Weight Loss

Within the following 12 to 24 hours your body will burn on average an extra 800 calories (varies person to person for an exact amount). So, by going in a Cryo Sauna for 3 minutes you will be burning an extra 800 calories and we all know how long that would take to burn off exercising!

However, it doesn't stop there, as the cold also speeds up your metabolic rate, so you are not only burning more calories, you're burning them more efficiently.

Happiness & Helping Depression

Put quite simply it just makes you feel better! A lot of the previous benefits overlap, it relaxes you, increases your production of endorphins and obviously, by getting a better night's sleep, it helps your mind and body repair which all lead to a reduction in depression and feeling happier.

Anti-Aging

We will cover anti-ageing from a looking younger perspective shortly, but this is from an anti-ageing perspective of you feeling younger and living longer. Cryotherapy does this by increasing your hormone production (these drop significantly as we age) which are key to a longer and better quality of life, combined with reducing your oxidative stress and not forgetting flushing out toxins within the body.

Plus, by feeling more relaxed, less depressed and ultimately less stressed, all keys to creating illnesses within the body, are now reduced which in turn, allows you to live better for longer.

According to the American Psychological Association, chronic stress is linked to the six leading causes of death: heart disease, cancer, lung ailments, accidents, cirrhosis of the liver and suicide. Do we need to say any more!

Beauty & Skin

One of the key components to amazing looking skin, is collagen. Cryotherapy increases your production of this wonder protein. Collagen is arguably the most important factors in great looking skin. This helps to make your skin thicker, tighter, in turn with less wrinkles and fine lines. The reduction of inflammation also makes your skin look brighter and more radiant.

Women have also reported cryotherapy has helped reduce their cellulite.

Pain Relief & Disease

For those suffering with chronic pain, cryotherapy can literally be a life line. The improvements have been shown to offer help to those suffering with arthritis, multiple sclerosis, fibromyalgia plus many more debilitating conditions. Though not a cure, it significantly helps with the pain associated with these conditions and helps improve the effects of these diseases. In Short, it reduces both pain and symptoms.

Popular Questions Asked About Cryotherapy

What is Cryotherapy?

Your body is exposed to a temperature of -110°C to -180°C. The treatment takes as little as 2 to 3 minutes, but the effect on the body is most spectacular. The extreme cold provides stimulus that activates physiological processes in the body. It's effectively like a system reboot of your body as the body scans itself for underperforming bodily functions and repairs itself rapidly.

How Will You Benefit from Cryotherapy?

The treatment is excellent as a supporting therapy for improving chronic pain, inflammation, itching and sports injuries. Also, the use of cryotherapy after an operation is quite common as it accelerates the healing process and improves any pain without high levels of medication and the accompanying side effects!

Professional athletes recover faster and perform at higher levels when cryotherapy is applied.

It's great for looking amazing as it improves the skins tone, texture and it tightens. For the body it can help you lose weight while simultaneously helping reduce cellulite. It's also excellent for helping with depression and moods.

How Does Cryotherapy Work Its Magic?

At -130°C, the temperature at the surface of your skin drops significantly to around freezing. This in turn activates your skin receptors (nerve endings) to start sending signals to the central nervous system, telling it that the body is in critical danger. Your body will immediately activate a wide range of defence processes which are really good for your well-being.

You will increase the production of serotonin, plus other endorphins which act as natural painkillers and feel-good hormones, your blood circulation will improve plus natural anti-inflammatories will also be activated and produced by the body.

This new increased level of oxygen and nutrient rich blood will help you rid your body of toxins and any metabolism residues. In a nutshell, the cold stimulus can be thought of as the body pressing a special button which activates a process creating a whole body readjustment and improvement.

How long will Your Treatment take?

Between 1 and 4 minutes generally.

Will You Need to Take Time Off Work?

No, you can go straight back to work afterwards.

Is Cryotherapy Safe?

Firstly - Cryotherapy has been safely used for over 30 years.

Secondly - We wouldn't personally use it ourselves every week if it wasn't!

That being said you will need to always follow the instructions carefully for your treatment. It's important your clothing is not wet or damp and that you are completely dry for your treatment, sensitive parts of the body are covered, and no metals are on your person whether in clothing or jewellery.

There Must Be Some Risk Though?

Cryotherapy is a relatively risk-free treatment provided the client has been assessed thoroughly beforehand. Blood pressure can rise, but this is only temporary.

There are a number of health conditions that exclude some people from the treatment, however most people can safely and effectively have cryotherapy. You must wear dry protective clothing including socks, underwear and gloves.

Is it Uncomfortable Being That Cold?

The very first time we had Cryotherapy we were all a touch nervous, and were most definitely thinking what must it feel like to be that cold, but really oddly it doesn't feel that bad, we have in fact felt colder stood in queues waiting to go into night clubs in our 20s!

A temperature of -180°C seems cold, however, remember the air in the chamber is extremely dry. Therefore, you do not really experience the cold as unpleasant. Plus, your only in there for, on average, 3 minutes...

How Often Should You Have Cryotherapy?

Obviously, this really depends on each individual person! However, once a week is a good starting point. For sports professionals, they may come in daily to speed up recovery and enhance strength and endurance while for someone who just wants to help with depression and feel better a few times a month is ideal.

How Much Does Cryotherapy Cost?

Cryotherapy represents excellent value for money due to the numerous cross benefits you get from having a treatment in addition to the primary reason why one chooses cryotherapy.

A typical treatment ranges from £50 to £75 however most providers offer discounts for multiple treatments or monthly plans.

Key Point

Although the use of cold has been around for centuries to help people recover from a range of conditions, cryotherapy provides the most effective and comfortable way for us to benefit from the vast array of benefits that the human body gets from being subjected to extreme cold.

You only have to ask yourself why Arsenal, Juventus, Everton, Leicester City, The Welsh Rugby team, Floyd

Mayweather plus the numerous other world class athletes all swear by it?

Chapter 26

Fat Freezing

When I first heard about this I was in my early 30s and though my stomach was still flat, I had this slight over hang at the sides when wearing certain shorts which I was not at all happy about!

This led me to do research into what could alleviate this concern of mine, as other than running 3 times a week for 20 minutes, I hated cardio and certainly wasn't going to be putting any more effort in, so how else was I going to get rid of these stubborn pockets of fat?

It also dawned on me if I had this problem then I bet others did!

It was at this point that I discovered fat freezing and what a discovery! This treatment is more aimed at pockets of fat than overall obesity. It goes about its magic in a very simple way. It just freezes the fat. This in turn kills the fat cells and then over the following weeks up to a third of fat in that area is gradually removed from the body via its natural processes.

It's that simple! In technical terms this process is called apoptosis, where a natural programmed cell death occurs because we have subjected the area to the cold for a certain amount of time and crystallised the targeted fat cells in the area we have treated.

Popular Questions Asked About Fat Freezing

Where does all the fat go?

Fat cells are simply destroyed and dissolved into the body and removed by its natural processes.

What are the after effects?

The reason fat freezing has become so popular is not just down to the excellent results it achieves, but that there are generally few side effects. No recovery period or downtime is required, and it is very rare to have extended redness or bruising post treatment.

In most cases, you are able to resume normal daily activities immediately after the session without discomfort, it's even possible to have a treatment on your lunch break!

How long does it take?

Each treatment takes up to 60 minutes per area, depending on the thickness of fat to be treated. Additional time may be required if you require more than one area. More powerful in-clinic machines can even perform two areas simultaneously to help make this a more profitable treatment for your clinic and double your rate of return per hour.

How many treatments are needed?

One session is sufficient for most people in most areas. Fat freezing has the advantage of not usually requiring a course of treatment. However, this obviously depends on the amount of fat you would like removed and the amount to begin with.

If your client's like the result and want to further improve on the result, you will have to wait at between 8 to 16 weeks before having another treatment.

Is it permanent?

Yes, the fat cells that will be crystallised through the fat freezing procedure are absorbed by the body's natural processes. Once destroyed the same fat cells can't grow back.

Is exercise required afterwards or any special diets?

No diets or intense exercise is needed post treatment. However, fat freezing is not a substitute for a healthy diet and exercise. After care includes increasing your water intake, plus avoiding caffeine and other toxins to support your body's natural processes.

Does it hurt?

The treatment for most is completely pain free and comfortable, some clients actually fall asleep during their treatment, like me!

How long does it take to see results?

This depends on the individual, the fat thickness, and the area treated. Changes happen over a number of weeks as the natural process happens, so some patience is required. Maximum results would be expected between 12 and 16 weeks, however some of our clients have noticed changes after only a week.

What areas can be treated?

In a nutshell, all those stubborn to remove fat areas such as:

- Inner and outer thighs
- Bingo wings/upper arms
- Upper and lower abdomen
- Man boobs
- Love handles and flanks
- Under bra back and side rolls
- Hips
- Buttocks

How much does a fat freezing treatment cost?

For one area prices start from £199 with certain high end clinics charging up to £1,995 for 3 areas.

Who can't be treated?

Fat freezing is suitable for the majority of people. However, you would not treat those pregnant or breastfeeding, circulatory issues and anyone with hernias or muscle weakness in the area to be treated, along with a few other health and safety aspects that would need to be checked prior.

The Difference Between Fat Loss and weight Loss?

It is a well known misconception that weight loss and fat reduction are the same thing, in fact they are not and never will be. When we loose weight from an area our fat cells become smaller but the actually number of fat cells remain the same, when we gain weight these fat cells become larger again and so the sequence follows throughout our lifetime, when we gain or loose weight.

What the fat freeze treatment does is remove the number of fat cells in the treated area therefore rather than just shrinking them to appear smaller like weight loss, we are in fact permanently removing them.

Key Point

For a long time clinics have concentrated on making the skin better with an anti-aging focus. However with the new range of body contouring treatments now available due to modern technology, allows you to fully profit from this exciting new area of treatments for an all over improved appearance, not just the face!

Chapter 27

Injectables

This is not something we have ever offered both from a training or treatment perspective so I am not the best versed to offer you advice on this subject however I do have some questions you need to ask yourself before or if continuing to offer fillers and muscle relaxants.

1. What are the long term effects on the muscle mass of your clients face having had the muscles relaxed and inactive for a long period of time, if used frequently?

2. Do the effects actually make your client look younger or just create less wrinkles?

3. Do the results bring attention to the fact your client has had a treatment?

4. Long term is this the best option for your client?

5. Does a shinny face look good and create a look of vitality for your clients?

6. Are your clients faces filled out too much that distort what they should look like?

7. Will over filled lips return back to normal, once the filler (and trend) has run its course? Or will be people be left with saggy lips!

Injectables can be profitable, particularly as it often turns into repeat business and is a quick fix for most, however a lot of thought needs to go into this area as to whether it's in your client's best interest or just your own bank accounts interest?

Finally, for those aestheticians not medically trained, now (January 2020) maybe the time to diversify into other non-surgical treatments, while you have the time to do this on your own terms, before the government take that decision away from you?

Chapter 28

The Oxygen Facial

The Oxygen Facial uses nature's most natural and essential key to life - Oxygen! This provides you with not just clear and radiant looking skin but also a younger fresher looking you.

It induces skin oxygenation to the skins surface layers, triggering an effect that brings oxygen to the face, which in turn is amazing for the skin, bringing much needed life and glow to your complexion.

At the same time, it also provides a fantastic deep exfoliating action to the surface of your skin, unblocking pores for clearer looking skin and especially great to help with your active acne and scarring!

I love this treatment so much for what it does to my skin and the radiant glow I get. After just my first treatment, I of course purchased one for home that I now use every fortnight. What's also not lost on me is that every time I have the treatment people approach me and comment on my skin.

Post exfoliation of your skin is now the optimal level time for the infusion of essential nutrients for you.

It also includes 4D Radio Frequency (RF), the RF allows this treatment to not just work at the top level of the surface, the epidermis, but get you even deeper into the dermis and create smoother, tighter skin, reducing your customers lines and wrinkles along with the sagging of the face.

An Oxygen Facial Will Help You:

1. Have a Radiant Glow!
2. Lift Your Face.
3. Hydrate and Plump Your Skin.
4. Tighten and Rejuvenate Your Skin.
5. Reduce Your Large Pores.
6. Help with Active Acne.
7. Reduce Wrinkles and Lines.

How Does The Oxygen Facial Do This?

It's a 4 Step Process:

1. Exfoliate the Skin.
2. Oxygenate the Skin.
3. Infuse the Skin.
4. Heat the Skin.

= Smooth + Tight + Glowing Looking Skin

Popular Questions Asked About

How Does The Oxygen Facial Work?

The Oxygen Facial uses the Bohr Effect, when CO_2 levels increase, the body needs to compensate, releasing oxygen from within to counteract the increased CO_2. This increased Oxygen is amazing for the skin providing a powerful and effective Oxygenation of your skin which in turn is amazing for anti-ageing and giving you the glowing look you've always desired.

Does it Hurt?

No, if anything it is soothing and most people find it relaxing.

Is The Oxygen Facial Safe?

Yes, it is non-invasive, and it's very minimal those that can't be treated by this.

Who is a Good Candidate For The Oxygen Facial?

Those suffering from acne, tired looking skin, generally run down or aged looking skin and those just wanting to look even better!

How Long Does an Oxygen Facial Treatment Take?

On average, it will take around 30 minutes.

How Many Oxygen Facial Treatments Will You Need?

This really does depend on the severity of the skin issue, a course of treatments will always yield more significant results than just a one off treatment. We would recommend one a week for four weeks, then once a fortnight on-going. The treatment results are visible almost immediately, even after just one treatment the skin will look noticeably better.

How Much Does The Oxygen Facial Cost?

Prices for a 30 minute session, start at £49 with discounts for a course of treatments. If combined with RF we recommend a price point of £99.

Are There Any Side Effects?

As long as all contra-indicators are carefully checked, no.

Key Point

This treatment is excellent if you're looking for an effective treatment that gives your clients an instant boost to how they look and feel, while providing you with excellent repeat business with customers initially coming back every week for the first month and thereafter every month!

Chapter 29

Hyperbaric Oxygen Therapy

For most people, their first reaction will be, "What the hell is this?" and for those of you familiar with what hyperbaric oxygen therapy (HBOT) is, will be thinking, "is this a diving book?".

Always being one of the first (if not the first) Aesthetic Trainers and Suppliers for any effective new natural treatment, plus the fun and enjoyment I personally get from researching and trying these things out on myself, it wasn't long before my research and trials would lead me to this fantastic treatment, hyperbaric oxygen therapy!

I'm sure you can guess what happened next... I bought a my very own! Which I have at home and can simply jump in anytime I want!

Why have we mentioned it in this book, a book that is focused on making your clinic more profitable? Well for exactly that reason. This treatment can make you money, and a lot of it. But more than that, it's simply magical what hyperbaric oxygen therapy can achieve for your clients.

HBOT has a huge array of proven benefits for what it can treat, however a lot of these are more medical based and this is a book about making your "aesthetic" focused clinic, more profitable. I will briefly touch below on the medical benefits it will bring anyone who uses a Hyperbaric Oxygen Chamber before focusing on why I am so very excited about this treatment and how it can be used for "Anti-Ageing" purposes.

What is HBOT and how does it work? In a nutshell, it provides your body and brain with more oxygen. At safe levels, more oxygen is amazing for us put quite simply!

The oxygen is delivered under increased pressure, combined with higher concentration of oxygen to your typical everyday levels. This places a higher level of oxygen in our bodies and more specifically in our blood. This in turn stimulates the growth of new blood vessels!

As you can imagine, with such significant effects on the body, this can help with the following:

- Carbon Monoxide poisoning
- Would Healing & Recovery from Injuries
- Brain Injury
- Multiple Sclerosis
- Strokes
- Diabetic Ulcers
- Slows cancer growths
- Autism

- Cerebral Palsy
- Obviously, what it's most famous for "The Bends" the infamous diving condition.

However, where I am really excited is what it does for those already healthy and wanting to improve themselves.

As we age everything slows down, and it's well considered that what is important and a huge influence on how quick we age is our DNA. Our DNA shortens as we get older, however when our DNA gets too short, they stop dividing and this is the key bit, we then stop getting new cell growth and division.

If you think of all the previous treatments mentioned some are working at the surface level on the epidermis e.g. Skin Micro Needling, some are going into the dermis e.g. Fractional Radio Frequency and more recent developments like High Intensity Focused Ultrasound (HIFU) are going really deep to the Superficial Muscular Aponeurotic System (SMAS). We often talk about beauty being just skin deep, well not anymore! HBOT is going super deep, into the very core of the human being and fixing the operating system that ages us!

Now surely, I hope you now can understand why I am so excited and bowled over by this treatment!

So, by using HBOT, we are potentially fixing the DNA that determines how we age. We are turning on the growth and repair hormone genes.

Other effects not related to aesthetics, but are still a huge pull for me, are the effects on the brain, users often report more energy in day to day life, plus a sharper and better functioning brain. If the brain can operate at higher levels for longer, this has to increase both quality of life and the desire to maintain a younger and healthier lifestyle, that in turn keeps you "looking younger than you should".

How will this make you money you're now probably asking yourself? Or when can I get one? Which is exactly what happened with me! Thoughts of generating money, when you realise what it can do for your own wellbeing soon vanish!

Quite simply you can charge your clients around £99 to come and use the hyperbaric oxygen chamber. This of course will create a very long and reliable income stream as you build up a strong following of people coming back time and time again! And of course, you get free use of an amazing treatment for yourself...

We have put together a guide for clinics who are considering offering Hyperbaric Oxygen Therapy called "Boost Your Business Out of Thin Air", if you would like a copy then please visit

The Profitable Clinic - The Skin Repair Group

www.theskinrepairclinic.co.uk/courses/hyperbaric-oxygen-therapy-chamber-business-packages/

However, a final word of warning, too much oxygen is bad for us. Too much oxygen will in fact cause us to over oxidise which we most certainly don't want, as this is very ageing. But like most things in life, the key to a successful result when using such great treatments is moderation!

Popular Questions Asked About HBOT

What Is It?

Hyperbaric oxygen therapy is a treatment that enhances the body's natural healing process by delivering oxygen under pressure, increasing the oxygen content in the blood and flooding the tissues with oxygen.

How Does Oxygen Therapy Work?

Oxygen Therapy works on 4 main levels. Hyperoxygenation, increases the oxygen dissolved in your bloods plasma (the liquid part of the blood), the oxygen dissolved in your lymphatic fluid, and the oxygen dissolved in your cerebrospinal fluid. Ultimately this means Oxygen Therapy increases the oxygen available to your body, so for damaged tissues, it's amazing for stimulating your healing.

Neovascularisation, Oxygen Therapy stimulates your

blood vessel formation and your collagen formation, this is what plumps out your skin and also your connective tissue in areas that were previously resistant due to lack of oxygen.

Hyperoxia enhanced antimicrobial activity, Oxygen Therapy reduces and/or eliminates the effects of toxic substances, bacteria, viruses, and yeast in your body by increasing the tissue's oxygen levels in your body.

Hyperoxia enhances immune response, Oxygen Therapy activates your white blood cells to help fight infections, promoting your resistance to infection, as well as wound healing. While also helping to reduce any inflammation and oxidative stress you may have.

What Does it Feel Like?

You will find it's very similar to flying. Clearing your ears will drastically help with your comfort levels. Once you have descended to relevant pressure and your ears adjust, you will feel completely normal in the chamber as you would when on a plane!

The great thing about this treatment is that you can simply sit or lie there and read, bring your laptop and work, use your ipod and watch films or surf the internet.

What Can Oxygen Therapy Treat?

Where do we begin! It can treat a huge variety of conditions however below are some of the most popular Oxygen Therapy is used for:

1. Increased Energy.
2. Improvement in Sleep.
3. Skin Conditions.
4. Anti-Ageing.
5. Wound Healing.
6. Cerebral Palsy.
7. Multiple Sclerosis.
8. Huntington's Disease.
9. Fibromyalgia.
10. Strokes.
11. ME.
12. Motor Neurone Disease.
13. Autism.
14. Rheumatoid Arthritis.
15. Ligament and Groin Strain.
16. Healing of Fractures.
17. AND There's More...

How Can Oxygen Therapy Treat Such A Wide Range of Conditions?

Simple as a lot of serious diseases/conditions come about from a lack of oxygen, so we are now simply removing the source of the problem by reintroducing higher levels of oxygen into the body.

When oxygen is restored to these tissues, much of the lost function returns. Oxygen Therapy also helps to reduce inflammation and promote wound healing throughout the body and even the brain.

Will You need to take time off work?

After your first treatment you may feel rather tired so we would recommend not having anything too demanding planned afterwards. There is no downtime. After your procedure you can resume your normal activities immediately, but avoiding anything too strenuous, without having to follow any special post-treatment measures. Clients can even have a session on their lunchbreak!

How Many Treatments Will You Need?

This all depends on what conditions you would like help with and the severity, however you will find once most people have had a few sessions and feel the huge benefits they get from it, they will be coming back weekly/monthly for a very long time to come.

Is it Safe?

Yes very, if administered carefully and correctly.

How long will the Treatment take?

Treatments start from 1 hour.

How much does the Treatment Cost?

The cost of an Oxygen Therapy Treatment starts from £99 for an hour.

Key Point

This is taking anti-ageing into the 22nd Century by going really deep. We are not just focusing on the skin, the external shield we project to the world, but making the brain younger and in turn our DNA more effective, to help us create and grow better quality cells as we get older.

This will certainly give your clinic the "WOW Factor" over your rivals and shows that you really are well ahead of the game, plus you can include some amazing PR angles here to really help get your clinic noticed.

Chapter 30

HIFE Accelerated Muscle Stimulation

Due to how amazing this treatment is, let's just hit you with the overwhelming facts from the get-go!

A HIFE treatment (short for High Intensity Focused Electromagnetic - yes, it's a mouthful and that's before you even add the AMS part...Accelerated Muscle Stimulation!) will deliver you 36,000 Sit-ups in 30 minutes, yes you did read that right!

I will also say it again... a 30-minute treatment recreates you performing 36,000 sit-ups. The HIFE device is truly game changing, both for your business and your body!

You're probably thinking two things now...where can I get one and I bet Ralph has one? Well the answer to the latter question, is of course he does (he also now seems to have more friends than before he bought it, odd that)!

This has to be one of the treatments I've been most excited for over the last two decades and that's a huge claim as if you speak to my best friend Gareth about our trip to Italy last summer, I wouldn't shut up about my Cryotherapy Chamber and how amazing it was, I even tried booking one while was away (they were fully booked for 2 weeks and we were only there a few days).

This technology is a huge cry from the original pioneering pads in the nineties, where you would stick them all over your body. In fact my dad still has his mini plastic suitcase stuffed full of these wires and pads behind some wardrobe.

What is High Intensity Focused Electro-Magnetic Accelerated Muscle Stimulation (HIFE-AMS)?

What everyone has always been wanting! It's a way to build muscle whilst simultaneously burning fat without enduring months in the gym.

The (very positive) side effect of this amazing level of muscle stimulation is that you also get to burn fat. So, it targets the two most important things people are wanting when it comes to their body, more muscle and less fat.

It works on the stomach for ripped abs, the arms for filling that sleeve or toning up the dreaded bingo wings, the thighs to help you get rid of wobbly bits while attaining the coveted thigh gap and where I feel the biggest shake up will be in this market is on the glutes for bum lifts.

Why? Well if you've been reading the trade press over the last few years this treatment could actually save lives as the Brazilian Bum Lift surgery is the most dangerous cosmetic surgical procedure in the world, with a reported death rate of 1 in 3,000 procedures.

This device will stop people even considering this option when they see the results obtained.

So, in a nutshell, we know the body is comprised of 35% muscle and now with HIFE Accelerated Muscle Stimulation device we have an effective way to build and strengthen the key areas of our body.

So How Does HIFE Do This??

A High Intensity Focused Electromagnetic workout is a non-invasive treatment of between 20-30 minutes that create a huge number of powerful muscle contractions, physically not possible through voluntary contractions.

When you are exposed to supramaximal contractions, your muscle tissue is now forced to adapt to these new extreme conditions you are being subjected to. Your body responds in a great way, creating a deep remodelling of its inner structure that results in you building muscle and burning fat.

HIFE has been approved by the FDA and can reduce the abdominal fat layer by 20% while increasing muscle mass by 18%.

HIFE fully activates your muscles in a way that exercise alone simply can't even get close to, which is how it achieves such an effective toning result in such a short period of time!

However, it doesn't stop there, it also has a separate action that breaks down your fat, so not only do you get bigger more toned muscle but you now will also be able to really see the new toned up muscles"

Popular Questions Asked About HIFE?

How Will HIFE Benefit Your Clinic?
The fact that this is not just another fat freezing or fat melting device means you open this treatment up to all those clients of yours that who perhaps have been too "thin" to warrant having a fat freezing treatment.

This increases your client based massively, well in fact to everyone now!

This will help you attract a new client base those, who wouldn't typically think to come to a clinic or salon for a treatment...

Who Will Your Customers Be for HIFE?
Anyone who wants to build toned muscle. Which is
pretty much all men and women aged 18 to 80!

Whether this is to give you your abs back, get a bum lift
or firm up your bingo wings (or in fact all of them!). This
will help you build muscle and burn with no sweat!

What Is HIFE?
A High Intensity Focused Electromagnetic workout is a
non-invasive treatment of between 20-30 minutes that
create a huge number of powerful muscle contractions,
physically not possible through voluntary contractions.

When we are exposed to supramaximal contractions,
our muscle tissue is now forced to adapt to these new
extreme conditions we are being subjected to. Your
body responds in a great way, creating a deep
remodelling of its inner structure that results in you
building muscle and burning fat.

How Long Will Your Treatment Take?

This will depend on the area to be treated, however
generally each treatment will 20 to 30 minutes, with a
minimum of 4 sessions scheduled two to three days
apart.

Will You Need to Take Time off Work?

There is no downtime. After your procedure, you can resume your normal activities immediately, without having to follow any special post-treatment measures. Clients can ever come to your clinic on their lunchbreak to have the treatment.

How Many Treatments Will You Need?

To see the great results we would expect, you will need a minimum of 4 sessions, scheduled two to three days apart.

What Does it Feel Like?

Interesting sums it up best as the HIFE treatment simply feels like an intensive workout. You can even lay back and relax during your treatment.

Who is a Good Candidate for a HIFE Treatment?

Anyone can benefit from HIFE if they are looking to increase muscle tone and reduce fat levels.

Is it Safe?

Yes very, it's the same as doing a super intensive work out at the gym but without the sweating!

How Long Does it Take to See Result?

You begin to feel results straight after your treatment. With visible improvements expected around two to four weeks after your last treatment, plus your results will continue to improve for several weeks following your treatment.

How Much Does a HIFE Treatment Therapy Cost?

A typical treatment averages around £495, with an average range of between £295 and £795.

Key Point

To sum this treatment up on one, would be "Game Changer". I'm sold as I've bought one for home, for my own personal use and as they say, the proofs in the pudding...

Chapter 31

Summary

Our objective for this book was to make your clinic more successful. We do believe summaries are very important to cement the ideas laid down in the preceding pages.

However, as valuable as summaries are, we wanted to make ours extra effective, so for that reason, rather than go over in brief detail all of the points previously mentioned, we decided to put together an action plan for you!

With a simple set of 20 action points, even if you can just perform one daily, every fortnight, within just a year, you would have transformed your clinic to a business you might not recognise. Whether this brings you more fun and enjoyment to the business or as the title suggests, more money, one thing we know, is that you will be more successful, however you choose to define success.

On a final note, we have thoroughly enjoyed writing this book as it cast our mind back to some interesting stages in my career and the numerous thoughts of "if only I knew that back then".

Thank you very much for reading and I am sure at some point in the future myself or The Skin Repair Group can be of help or assistance to you.

Ralph Montage,
The Skin Repair Group.

Chapter 32

Your Checklist for Success...

You have taken your first steps to improving your business by reading this book but without action all this will be in vain.

For that reason, we have put together a clear and precise summary of what you need to do, into an actionable format to make it as easy as possible for you to get the basics implemented and implemented now.

If you would like to download a free easy to use version of this for your clinic then please simply visit: www.theprofitableclinic.co.uk/free-bonus-gifts.

1. **Are you calling back all enquiries within 24 hours and preferably the same day of enquiries?**
   a. If not, what member of staff can you make available to do this?
   b. Is it worth employing and extra member of staff to just deal with incoming enquiries on a full time basis?
   c. If there is not enough work for this then consider a part time employee if no-one you have is currently suitable.

2. Do you have 3 price points for all treatments?

a. If not design 3 packages priced low - to initially attract, priced mid point - what most people will buy, and then priced at high point - those who have the best of everything will go for, this option where you make the highest margins.

3. Are you currently taking deposits?
a. If not, ensure you take 50% deposit using your card machine, however while you're getting more comfortable with this process perhaps start off at just 25%.

4. After EVERY treatment are your staff rebooking your customer back in before they leave your clinic?
a. If not, ensure ALL your staff ask to rebook your customer in, straight after and before they have left along with taking a 25-50% deposit for this.

5. Do you know your Gross Profit per treatment? Just because you are taking £100 an hour from customers, doesn't mean you're making £100 an hour profit.
a. If not, calculate what your gross profit per treatment is.
b. For those who want to be ahead of their game you could even calculate your net profit by apportioning fixed overheads relevant to your treatment.

6. **Are you filling up set days first, or trying to just fit your customer in when it's convenient for them?**
   a. If so, this is wrong for the success of your business. Until you are full select 3 days a week to focus on, once full, then open up extra days.

7. **Do you ask your customer when booking them in, when they would like to have their treatment?**
   a. If so, stop from now on when booking customers in, only do so on the days you have available appointments before opening up new treatment days!

8. **When was the last time you put your prices up?**
   a. If the answer is over a year ago, it's time to put them up NOW, Today! Aim at least 15% and for some try 25%. You will be surprised at how little it affects sales after the odd initial moan and you might even be able to start offering even more to your customer.

9. **Are you asking every enquiry if they would like to book their treatment when on the phone with them?**
   a. If so, make sure you give the potential client, 3 date options of when to come in and not just ask, "when's good for you"?

10. **Less is more, are you offering too many treatments? Are you able to service the treatments to the standard you would like?**
    a. If not, drop the least profitable ones whether that based on a per hour use of your time or the total revenue it brings in per month/annum.

11. **How many times are you calling back an enquiry? Just once?**
    a. If so, you need shooting!
    b. You need to call back every enquiry at least 5 times however we in fact will call an enquiry back 8 to 10 times before deleting the enquiry.

12. **Are you booked up 4 weeks in advance?**
    a. If no, then you have too many staff. Only recruit extra aestheticians when you reach this critical point.

13. **Do you have videos of your clinic on your website, social media etc.?**
    a. If not, you need in the next month to have videos filmed of all your treatments, your clinic with some/all of the staff and premises proudly on show.
    b. You should get into the habit of filming reviews of delighted customers after their treatments!

14. **Website's the Basic's**
    a. Go back and review the checklist in Chapter 14.

15. Can you describe who your typical client is? In detail!

    a. You need to be able to describe things such as relationship, age bracket, do they have children, their income, concerns they have in life, professions, their lifestyle, what things they enjoy, what else do they spend their money on, role models in life…

    b. Once you know this, you can tailor all your marketing and services with these people in mind, in order to attract more of them!

16. Do you have a record of every single client you ever had?

    a. If no, you need to get your least busy member of staff to enter all those thousands of consent forms into a spreadsheet or CRM system so that you have backups and equally important you can get in touch with them, promoting things of interest to them throughout the year.

17. Do you offer those little extra's to your clients? Such as:

    a. Offer them a drink when come into the clinic?

    b. Return all calls within 24 hours?

    c. Always greet clients with a smile?

    d. Offer to take their coat?

    e. Provide interesting reading material while they wait?

18. **Honestly ask yourself what are the first impressions people are having of my clinic?**
    a. Are the premises clean and clear of clutter?
    b. From outside does the clinic look inviting?
    c. Are the colours bright, fresh and a nice place to be?
    d. Refer to Chapter 18 for my detailed checklist but until the above are done, don't waste your time!

19. **Do people like you and your staff?**
    a. If not, you have a huge problem which is probably already apparent by the lack of money in your bank account.
    b. Remove any staff that bring a bad attitude to your business TODAY.

20. **Do you want to run your business forever?**
    a. If not, which of course is probably the case, you need to think about how you are to sell your business, when the time is needed so that everything is already in place.

Chapter 33

About The Skin Repair Group

Setup over a 15 years ago in 2005, the business started off just offering treatments. The business then expanded to 3 clinics a few years later. In 2010 the first training courses for Skin Micro Needling were launched using the roller and the pen device.

Even having been around for some time (only invented by the Egyptians!), skin micro needling in 2010 was relatively unheard of. It was only in 2012 when micro needling with both the roller and pen device really took off. We then decided to close one of the clinics to concentrate more on training and business packages (equipment supply).

Having already offered fat freezing and fractional radio frequency in the clinics for some time, they made for the obvious choice for the next round of training courses to be developed. In turn High Intensity Focused Ultrasound (HIFU) was introduced, along with the Oxygen Facial and HIFE Accelerated Muscle Stimulation devices a few years later.

In 2018 with Ralph realising he would be 40 soon, the business further expanded to focus on both anti-aging and longevity treatments in order to help our clients both live longer and better for longer. This led us to start offering Hyperbaric Oxygen Chambers, Cryotherapy Chambers and Localised Cryotherapy.

What makes us truly different to others is opposed to traditional device suppliers whereby you get a bit of training bolted on when you buy a device, The Skin Repair Group offer complete Business Packages, which are exactly what they say they are!

Comprehensive packages whereby we train you, we provide you with the equipment, all the consumables to operate the device PLUS we give you a complete business, marketing and sales program, *"The Triple P Program"* that's 57 modules of everything you need to know and action to make your Clinic Profitable.

Other support includes things such as:

1. How to setup your company website.
2. How to register your company.
3. Becoming VAT registered.
4. Getting the right insurance for you.
5. What qualifications you need and how to get them?
6. How to make sure you don't fail.
7. How can you get lots of customers?
8. Ensure you get great results from the treatments you offer.
9. Marketing material designed for you to use with access to flyers, business cards and posters.

10. Lots of Before and After photographs ready for you to use from day one.
11. Videos of all the treatments and video FAQs for your clients to watch.
12. Sales support.
13. Sourcing and booking treatments in for your clinic, however this is location dependant.

It doesn't stop there however as:

- We can even come to you, so your training can take place at your clinic! No long journeys and getting lost trying to find us (you are more than welcome to come to us if you want however).
- Ongoing and unlimited technical advice forever for all business packages purchased.
- All the up-to-date consent forms and after care sheets already done for you, providing you with complete treatment packs for your clients.
- Comprehensive back up and support for all your equipment purchased.
- We're always on the lookout for the latest cutting-edge technology so that you can offer your clients the world's best longevity and anti-aging treatments and importantly stay ahead of your competition.

If you're looking to offer exciting new treatments for your customers then we would be delighted to help in any way we can to make your clinic, a profitable one.

Visit our website:

www.theskinrepairgroup.com

Some of you may prefer to pick up the phone and we very much welcome phone enquiries:

0203 519 2525.

We look forward to helping you at some point in the future.

Ralph & Alexandra,

The Skin Repair Group.

Chapter 34

About the Author, Ralph Montague

Ralph setup his first aesthetic clinic in 2005 having experienced first-hand the difficulties of running a clinic, so much so in fact, that it wasn't long before unfortunately he had to return to the world of the employed, operating the business on a part time basis.

With time came extensive and profitable learnings, enabling Ralph a second time round to go full time with the business and with some of the simple guidance and steps contained in this book he was able to not just get by but flourish with a regional chain of clinics!

Ralph is founder and was previously Managing Director of The Skin Repair Clinic, a regional chain of aesthetic clinics. Now a Director of The Skin Repair Group, a national training and equipment supplier, offering the most comprehensive business advice for clinic owners (and aspiring clinic owners), technical support and cutting-edge machines to help clinics maximise their profits. Specialising in:

- High Intensity Focused Ultrasound (HIFU).
- Fat Freezing.
- Oxygen Facials.
- Skin Micro Needling (The Skin Repair Pen).
- Cryotherapy Chambers.
- Localised Cryotherapy.
- HIFE Accelerated Muscle Stimulation.
- On-line marketing & business workshops.

Having helped thousands of clinics over the years, combined with now approaching two decades worth of knowledge and experience, The Profitable Clinic series of books came about by lots of customers asking for the same advice time and time again.

Which made it a simple decision to put pen to paper (well fingers to keys!) to create this comprehensive business book to making your clinic both a success and profitable.

On the back of The Profitable Clinics success, Ralph has recently put together the world's most comprehensive business program for Clinics looking to be more Profitable!

"The Triple P Program" covers the key elements to any clinic's success profitability. Promote. Profit. Protect.

Each P being a 90-day program to drive clinic owners to create the lives they've always dreamed of.

Ralph certainly practices what he preaches, having a Cryotherapy Chamber, a Localised Cryotherapy Device, a Hyperbaric Oxygen Chamber, an Oxygen Facial Device, a Skin Repair Pen and his most recent addition the HIFE Accelerated Muscle Stimulation device, all at home for his personal use.

Further books are planned on the topics of anti-aging and longevity, once we've hit our targets to help 10,001 UK clinic owners become more profitable...

If you would like to know more about how Ralph can help make your clinic more profitable, please feel visit www.theprofitableclinic.co.uk.

Wishing you all a Very Profitable Clinic.

Ralph Montague.

THE PROFITABLE CLINIC PRESENTS THE FULL RECORDING OF THE VIRTUAL WORKSHOP FOR CLINIC & SPA OWNERS...

The Essential Steps YOU can take TODAY to make your clinic more PROFTIABLE, broken down into quick, simple and easy to follow bites for you!

During this fact filled workshop, The Profitable Clinic author, Ralph Montague, will be sharing the essential steps you need to take your business (right now!) to build the basics AND protect yourself from the economic madness that we are about to enter.

What You'll Discover:

- ✓ **The Key QUICK Wins** - Simple ways to get MORE bookings, to sail the stormy seas ahead.
- ✓ **Multiple FREE Sales Steps** - That you can use to generate a surge of cash in your business.
- ✓ **The Cash Management Foundations** - Why CASH is King and ways that won't cost you anything but will lead to more money in your bank account
- ✓ **Decisive Action Plans** - Done for you planning and checklists to ensure the survival of your business.
- ✓ **And Much, Much MORE!**

The Profitable Clinic - The Skin Repair Group

Yes, I Want to Make My Clinic More Profitable - If so Visit
www.theprofitableclinic.co.uk

What is The Profitable Clinic Workshop?

The workshops are the exact same Profitable Clinic Workshops we offer live throughout the world and is just like an in-person event, just delivered virtually via videos. This isn't a webinar, it's a proper real event and was an entire day filming to get this ready for you with content sessions, you can take breaks whenever you want and even watch it from the comfort of your own home without extensive travelling and expensive hotels!

Watch this Virtual Workshop Today - Visit
www.theprofitableclinic.co.uk

Why Any Smart Business Owner MUST Watch This Workshop?

Most things in life are simple however it does take time to experience these things and therefore learn from these simple things. What if you could tap into someone else's mistakes and learnings of almost two decades and steal their "knowledge" in an instant and use it for yourself now, TODAY?

Getting and keeping customers is going to be more challenging now, more than ever.

The Profitable Clinic - The Skin Repair Group

Thousands of people will lose their jobs, thousands of businesses will close their doors, the economists say we've already entered the next recession and it's crucial that as small business owners, the backbone of the economy, we do all we can to not just survive this impending storm but thrive in it. And that's exactly what The Profitable Clinic Workshops are all about.

Yes, I Want to Make My Clinic More Profitable - If so Visit
www.theprofitableclinic.co.uk

How many times can I watch it again?

LOADS! You will have free access to The Profitable Clinic Workshop for whenever you want, so you can dip in and out of it as many times as you like, again and again in the future, whether it's to tweak certain parts of your business or if you just need to be reminded of everything now and again.

How much is it?

This workshop event in person is normally £295 however we are offering it as a virtual workshop for just £97, so a MASSIVE £200 saving for you PLUS it gets "even better", enter code TPC and it will be just 77, so you get the entire recording of the FULL Days workshop all for just 77.

How do I access The Profitable Clinic Workshop?

Visit www.theprofitableclinic.co.uk

- hydrate
- Toner
- gel facmer
- Tpcd
- cleen
- Treim 1

Cleenser 53.96
Toner → 37.54
Densueen → 65.86
Cleen → 117.08
Isotretinin → 98.86
hydrate → 74.7s

Printed in Great Britain
by Amazon

48703981R00119